GARY SPEED

UNSPOKEN

THE FAMILY'S **UNTOLD** STORY

JOHN RICHARDSON
WITH LOUISE SPEED

Reach Sport

*'Maybe it was something Gary
lived with all his life, especially after
re-reading some of his early letters.
He was able, perhaps, to control it by
being so in control of his life...
I don't think Gary would have
been able to express a weakness
to me. He was the one everyone
else would go to'*

Louise Speed

37 KENTMERE AVE
SEACROFT
LEEDS

Dear Louise,

I don't really know what to
say. I have been thinking about finishing
at Leeds, I've also been thinking of other
things which I won't say. I'm so
depressed. I'm just going to go to
sleep now and hope I never wake up.
I love you so much, I will always
love you.

I don't know what else to say
except you might see me sooner than
you think, or otherwise. You never leave
my mind, nothing else seems to matter
anymore, I love you more than
you can imagine,

Gary
xxx

A letter 17-year-old Gary wrote to Louise

ABOUT THE AUTHOR

 John Richardson has worked on national newspapers for more than 30 years, including two spells on the Daily Mail, and for 16 years he was the chief football correspondent for the Sunday Express. He has also been a regular contributor to Sky Sports' Sunday Supplement programme and has appeared on beIN SPORTS, LFC TV and MUTV.

John was the ghostwriter for Terry McDermott's autobiography, *Living For The Moment*, and also helped maverick Wales star Mickey Thomas put together his colourful life story in *Kick-Ups, Hiccups, Lock-Ups*.

He also upset Sir Alex Ferguson, just plain Alex at the time, after he and several national newspaper colleagues were given permission by Wales boss Terry Yorath to interview Ryan Giggs. The red mist descended on the Manchester United manager, who until then had successfully kept the young Giggs away from all interview requests. Seeing Giggs spread over several national newspapers sent the protective Ferguson into a frenzy and assured this author of a blast of the renowned 'hairdryer'!

I would like to dedicate this biography to Gary's wife Louise, sons Ed and Tommy, parents Roger and Carol, and sister Lesley.

A special thanks to Louise, who has played a large part in what was obviously a painful exercise in revisiting the past but has given unwavering support to the project.

Amongst the tears there have also been plenty of laughs recalling some of their happy times together after first meeting at school. Without Louise's blessing this book wouldn't have been undertaken.

Also a big thank you to all those who have given up their time to speak about someone who meant so much to them, even if at times it reawakened the heartbreaking memories of his passing.

Finally, thanks to my wonderful wife Sue, who has been alongside me supporting me all the way on what has been at times an emotional roller-coaster but hopefully offers a unique insight into a life so tragically cut short.

Hopefully it is both enjoyable and poignant.

John Richardson

Reach Sport

www.reachsport.com

Written by John Richardson. With thanks to Louise Speed.

Paperback first published in Great Britain and Ireland in 2019
by Reach Sport, 5 St Paul's Square, Liverpool, L3 9SJ.
Hardback first published in 2018.

www.reachsport.com
@reach_sport

Reach Sport is a part of Reach plc.
One Canada Square, Canary Wharf, London, E15 5AP.

1

Paperback ISBN: 9781911613312.
Hardback ISBN: 9781910335932.
eBook ISBN: 9781911613121.

Photographic acknowledgements:
Louise Speed's personal collection,
Mirrorpix, PA Images.

Design and typesetting by Reach Sport.
Jacket design: Rick Cooke. Book editing: Harri Aston.
Career statistics sourced from Gary Speed Remembered: A Celebration
Of A Life In Football, copyright Paul Abbandonato

Printed and bound by CPI Group (UK) Ltd, Croydon, CR0 4YY.

CONTENTS

Introduction by author John Richardson   11

1. **Gary's story: The autobiography**
   It's a park life   25
2. **Louise's story:**
   How we fell in love   39
3. **Friends' story:**
   Kevin Ratcliffe   51
   Howard Wilkinson   57
   Simon Grayson   65
   Mickey Thomas   72
   Chris Kamara   79
4. **Louise's story:**
   Our life as a family   87
5. **Friends' story:**
   Bobby Gould   101
   Joe Royle   106
   Barry Horne   110
   John Hartson   113
   Ian Rush   120
   Robbie Savage   126
   Neville Southall   132

6. **Gary's story: The autobiography**
   Tyne to move   141

7. Louise's story:
    Picking up the pieces   157

8. Friends' story:
    Shay Given   165
    Craig Bellamy   175
    Steve Harper   184
    Terry McDermott   188
    Bryn Law   194
9. Parents' story:
    Never at peace   205
10. Friends' story:
    Kevin Nolan   217
    Osian Roberts   223
    Chris Coleman   231
    Dan Walker   239
    Matt Hockin   243
11. Louise's story:
    Finding a way through   253

In his own words   261
Tributes to Speedo   265
A glittering career   273
Heads Together   286
A note from CALM   288

Introduction

THE UNTOLD STORY

*Author John Richardson reveals how he was given
the job of writing Gary's autobiography and why
the time is right to complete the story with help from
wife Louise, close family, friends and colleagues from
Gary's remarkable footballing life*

It came out of the blue in the midst of a telephone conversation as Gary – or Speedo as he was affectionately known throughout football – was winding his way back to his Chester home from south Yorkshire where he was a manager with Sheffield United.

"I've been thinking about writing a book about my life and career so far and I'd like you to help me with it," he asked as he negotiated one of the many hairpin corners on the Snake Pass.

I quickly joked that if he didn't pay due attention to the picturesque but dangerous road which crosses the Peak

District as part of his daily journey I'd be writing the book by myself.

"Okay," he agreed. "We'll have a proper chat later in the week in the Grosvenor Arms."

This was our favoured drinking hole close to his home on the outskirts of Chester and only a few further miles from my base.

After putting the phone down I felt I was walking on air. Had I heard right? An absolute icon of the game, hugely respected by his peers, wanted me to become, in effect, his ghostwriter?

It turned out he had been approached by a leading publisher which had obviously decided there was a market out there ready to devour tales of Speedo's career. Typically, the idea hadn't originated from Speedo himself, a paragon of humility who was never one to seek the headlines.

That was another reason for me feeling 10 feet tall because, although he was always helpful and courteous, he wouldn't go out of his way to socialise with sports journalists.

We'd hit it off though, initially through spending time together with Wales. At first it was purely a professional relationship where Speedo would make himself available for interviews, always acknowledging you had a job to do.

Initially, as one of the younger players in the squad, he was a little withdrawn, eyeing your movements and analysing how the older players like Ian Rush, Kevin Ratcliffe, Mark Hughes, Neville Southall and Dean Saunders dealt with the media, and if they appeared happy dealing with you then Speedo would slowly drop his guard.

Thankfully for me, I'd been accepted by the main men who had quickly realised that outside working hours it was a case of enjoying yourself as much as possible, which usually involved a bar of some description.

This was an era when there were no mobile phones ready to recall at an instant any misdemeanour, a time when the media and players mixed freely and there was absolute trust.

Many a blind eye was turned on the nocturnal goings-on of both parties. It was in this laissez-faire environment where professional relationships could develop into genuine friendships. That was the case with myself and Speedo, especially with Wales' away trips affording you plenty of time for conversations. Safe to say in his formative years representing his country the travel arrangements of the Football Association of Wales were more Fawlty Towers than Thomas Cook.

Always ones for cutting costs, it was never the quickest route to the far-flung destinations of World Cup or European Championship qualifiers. Marco Polo, the renowned 13th century traveller, could have got to some places quicker. Imagine England players being asked for a show of hands for the pilot to know whether he should make a second attempt to land at a foggy Faroe Islands after an aborted first effort, or being asked in Moldova to board a bullet-ridden, war-torn coach.

But incidents like these brought everyone together, forging a unique bond between the travelling media and Wales players.

The bond was tested somewhat on a trip to Cyprus when, trying to find our way inside the stadium, we were stopped by an official who asked who we were and where were we trying to get to. Back came the reply from the *Daily Telegraph* representative: "We're the English press". Suddenly, the booming voice of the Welsh-speaking and former Wales keeper Dai

Davies, who was part of the media group, yelled out: "No, we're f*****g not, we're the bloody Welsh press!"

The laughter which followed proved no harm was done and very quickly the story filtered its way down to some of the players, including Speedo, who was quick to ask before any subsequent interviews whether he was talking to the English or the Welsh press!

As he grew older he became more and more relaxed dealing with any media duties and he encouraged me to keep in touch away from Wales duty – an absolute godsend for a football writer because the snippets of information you would pick up in various conversations would be transformed into stories for the newspaper.

I'd not really known Speedo during his early days at Leeds United, where under Howard Wilkinson he picked up a First Division championship winning medal – the last season before the Premier League was launched.

But from afar you could see how talented he was, a vital cog in the midfield which also comprised David Batty, Gordon Strachan and Gary McAllister. The fact Howard Wilkinson named him as his player of the year in the all-conquering season illustrated the exciting career which lay ahead of him.

Despite his film-star looks – it was never wise to be photographed next to him – there was never any signs of vanity or aloofness as he climbed the football ladder.

Often in later years, when we met up for a quick drink or chat, he would be recognised and any requests for an autograph or photo were politely granted without any fuss. Nothing was too much trouble.

As Speedo and I grew closer, so did the trust and we would speak off the record on many subjects. I would only use in print what he wanted out in the public domain, which was frustrating at times because as a journalist you can foresee the headlines of a potentially excellent story for the back pages.

One of the most frustrating times I believe for both of us was the vitriol which came his way after leaving his boyhood team Everton for Newcastle United.

He, like all the players, loved the legendary manager Howard Kendall but "there was a cloud hanging over the dressing room – one I couldn't accept – and so I left."

As he explained in one of the chapters for the original autobiography (more of that later), the main reason for his departure had never been told.

He was accused of being a traitor – and worse – by many incensed supporters who weren't aware of what was going on behind the scenes at Goodison Park.

"I was public enemy number one as far as the Everton fans were concerned for some time," he told me. "In a way I was glad to see Nicky Barmby move across Stanley Park from Everton to Liverpool because that took some of the heat off me."

We are reproducing the chapter that emerged from those discussions but even then Speedo stopped short of graphically stating his reasons for cutting short his stay at the club he had supported from the terraces. All I could push him on was revealing that the manager's physical state wasn't the best and, as a professional footballer, he couldn't accept that.

Never once did he come out and say, despite all the abuse and threats which came his way, that in fact Howard was battling with a drink problem. I kept prompting him when we were in the process of putting his book together that this was finally the time to put the record straight.

He wouldn't but I have because his memory doesn't deserve to be tarnished in any way and, in any case, most people in the game knew of Howard's over-indulgence in alcohol. That hasn't diminished in any shape or form the love which is still felt for Everton's most successful manager.

So for those who abused Speedo at the time, and anyone still mystified by his determination to leave Everton for Newcastle, here it is – he left because he had lost respect for his manager and found it hard to continue playing under him.

Never once when he was under fire from angry Everton fans did he ever succumb and defend himself with the real reason for his disillusionment at Goodison Park. That takes guts and now I believe he deserves the truth to come out.

I can hear him now, almost certainly remonstrating with me, that he didn't want this to become public knowledge.

Nothing though deserves to stain a wonderful career, one which also took in Newcastle United, Bolton and Sheffield United.

Sadly, he was never able to expand on some of the topics we touched on as between us we pieced together a synopsis for the original book.

Gazing over pages and pages of notes, I'm sure he wouldn't mind you having an insight into what would have eventually been produced – even though he constantly worried about whether he had done enough in his life to make the book interesting.

Thanks to those who have contributed to this book with some of the tales about Speedo. For me it was just a case of filling in some of the cracks.

At Leeds he went on to have a great relationship with Wilkinson – but that wasn't the case early on. He admitted he was petrified when, as a young player, Wilko threw a shirt at him and "wiped the floor with me" after a poor display. "Some of the seasoned pros at Leeds came up to me later to offer me some sympathy," Speedo told me. "It didn't stop me being bombed out of the first team for four or five games though."

As we discover from a number of people, he learned a lot from the more experienced Gordon Strachan, on and off the pitch. "Gordon would run the Leeds show on the wing, often refereeing games at the same time," he told me. But it was his knowledge about fitness and the body which left the biggest impression on a young Speedo.

He hailed Wilkinson for bringing in Eric Cantona, which had the effect of giving the side extra impetus on their way to landing the First Division title.

The next season proved to be a huge contrast as Leeds finished 17th and were not able to win a single away game. Cantona left for Manchester United and Gary revealed that many of the players felt Wilko "had lost his marbles" when he came up with stats which illustrated that Leeds lost more games with Cantona in the side.

There was also huge drama in the European Cup. In the tie with Stuttgart, Leeds lost 3-0 but won 4-1 at Elland Road, only to go out on away goals. "We were reprieved when it was discovered Stuttgart had fielded an ineligible player. We played a third game in Barcelona's Nou Camp stadium and won 2-1."

But there was to be no reprieve in the so called 'Battle Of Britain'. "Gary McAllister momentarily silenced the Ibrox crowd but we went out over the two legs to complete a miserable season," Speedo told me, gloomily.

He spoke briefly of the end of his time at Leeds. "I couldn't believe it when, in the League Cup quarter-final against Aston Villa, Howard abandoned the normal 4-4-2 system and went for 5-3-2, which saw me operate as a left wing back. We ended up getting hammered."

Then there was the day he went into Wilko's office to be told there was a new contract for him. It was in an envelope. "I could only open it if I committed to stay. I still don't know what it said because I said I was leaving."

It was assumed that it was all cut and dried for him to join his boyhood team Everton, who had just won the FA Cup.

"Newcastle were also in for me," he explained. "There was a real temptation to join them because under Kevin Keegan everything was happening on Tyneside. But he wanted me to play as a left-back and I didn't fancy that."

Ironically, his first game for Everton was against Newcastle, who had signed Alan Shearer – later to become a huge mate – for a world record fee of £15 million. "We won 2-0 and I scored the second goal."

At the Magpies he witnessed the fall-outs between Ruud Gullit, who succeeded Dalglish as manager, and Alan Shearer and Rob Lee. These flashpoints contributed to Gullit leaving. "Ruud though was technically one of the best coaches I've worked under," he revealed.

He spoke about Roy Keane's snarling accusations that Speedo went out nobble him in the FA Cup final. "Keano's replacement Teddy Sheringham went on to score one of the goals as we lost 2-0!"

With Gullit gone, Bobby Robson helped heal the divisions, illustrated when Shearer scored five times in an 8-0 thrashing of Sheffield Wednesday.

At the beginning of the 2004-05 season it started unravelling for Gary at Newcastle.

"During a pre-season tournament in Hong Kong I received a phone call telling me Newcastle had accepted a £750,000 bid from Bolton for me," he explained.

"I found out the chairman Freddy Shepherd wanted to bring in Nicky Butt from Manchester United. Bobby Robson didn't know a thing about it. I told him I couldn't play in the tournament game because I was off to Bolton. He named me as one of the substitutes and I ended up scoring one of the penalties as we won on spot-kicks."

Gary went to play under Sam Allardyce at Bolton, Big Sam using Speedo as a sounding board when Newcastle wanted Allardyce as their new manager.

Later, it was on to Sheffield United, with Speedo prepared to drop down a division. He was 38, after all.

He always possessed the human touch and it was no surprise when his majestic playing career came to an end that he would quickly switch successfully to coaching and management.

Sheffield United, his final club, had seen his coaching potential and at Bramall Lane he then moved into the management chair vacated by Kevin Blackwell.

It was then that we started on his autobiography, Speedo

having insisted to the publishers that he wanted me as the ghostwriter, someone he felt comfortable with in the countless hours it would take to record his life story. Gary and his wife Louise had also been among the guests who celebrated my wedding with wife Sue on an evening cruise along Chester's River Dee – both of them being subjected to many photo requests as the star couple.

So, Dictaphone and notebook in hand, I'd meet up with Speedo, usually over a drink and sandwich in the Grosvenor Arms, and we'd start reliving his life and wonderful career. But without fail the conversation would have to come to an abrupt stop as he would leave to pick up his two boys, Tommy and Ed. He absolutely doted on them and there was no way he would allow himself to be late. The book could wait.

Then one day, completely out of the blue, again as he made his way from Sheffield to home, he announced he didn't want to continue with the book. "I don't think I've done enough to warrant a book," he told me.

Obviously it was up to him but I told him I felt he was being too hard on himself and the synopsis we were working on ran to three large pages, one which had certainly satisfied the demanding publishers who don't commission books for the sake of it.

But no amount of counter-arguments were going to change his mind so I agreed, reluctantly, to leave it in abeyance until he felt the time was right to bring his book out.

The regular chats still continued though and soon he was appointed manager of Wales, one of his proudest moments. "That's another chapter for the book," I quipped.

He was determined to change the face of Welsh international

football, which had sunk to a low ebb, although it wasn't long before he was immersed in FAW politics, which have blighted many of his predecessors' ambitions. Just a week before his death, Speed rang me and told me he'd had enough and was thinking about resigning. There was a bit of noise coming down the phone and so I asked him where was he speaking from.

"I'm in the Trafford Centre [Manchester] shopping with Louise," he replied. I told him he would have to go shopping every day if he quit as Wales manager. He laughed and added: "Maybe I'll have a rethink!"

That was my last conversation with someone who I now regarded as a mate. I can still hear that Speedo chuckle now – infectious, typical of the person I had got to know over the years. Then came the telephone call, from a national newspaper colleague, which left me shattered and bewildered.

I was in the car with my wife travelling to my father-in-law's. I answered the call and it was Chris Bascombe of the *Daily Telegraph*.

"Look," he said. "I don't want to worry you because you know what rumours are like but there's something I think you should know. It's about Gary Speed and I wouldn't have rung you but I've heard this now from a couple of people."

I wondered why he was being so nervous – he was obviously going to tell me that Speedo had quit as Wales manager. It wasn't any great shock.

What followed was and it was a wonder the car stayed on the road.

"I'm sorry to tell you but it's going around that Speedo has been found hanged," Chris told me.

I didn't believe it. "It's just a sick rumour," I told him. If I had been told Speedo had been killed in a car accident or something like that, it would still have been a shock but I would have believed it. But to hang himself, no way.

I thought I'd ring a mutual mate, Ian Rush, another great Wales international. It was a foreign ringtone but he answered pretty quickly.

"Where are you?" I enquired. "In Dubai," he answered. "Have you heard these rumours about Speedo?" I continued.

There was then an eerie silence. Neither of us knew what to say. I just mumbled about speaking to him later. I just felt physically sick – none of this made sense. I'd lost my mother just a few months earlier but she was 86 and had dementia, Speedo was 42 and always looking the epitome of good health.

There was only one thing for it. Ring him and pray he answers to nail the rumours. His phone was ringing out – any moment now I'd hear his voice chortling about the stories flying around about him. Instead it went to voicemail and so I left a message for him to ring me back as quickly as possible.

Of course, the call never came and a bright light had gone out in the world. But almost seven years later, maybe we can bring part of that light back with a celebration of his life through the book he was going to write.

As some sort of comfort, from time to time I have pulled the original two chapters from one of my drawers together with the synopsis which was going to shape the direction of the book.

Now, for the first time, you will be able to read those chapters while the synopsis has been turned around with some of the people who were going to form important parts of his life story, revealing their thoughts and poignant tales connected to Speedo.

This book wouldn't have been complete without the involvement of Louise who, despite the pain of her terrible loss, has spared the time to talk about and provide a powerful insight into life with Gary. I also know it was very difficult for Carol and Roger Speed to talk openly about the wonderful son they lost too soon. But through a mixture of laughter and tears they have added to the heartfelt celebration of his life.

None of us can ever bring him back but hopefully the following pages will help him live on in our memory.

1

Gary's story

The autobiography

IT'S A PARK LIFE

'Kids can be cruel and I was left in no doubt from some of them about what they thought of me coming from the rival school. It got so bad sometimes that I would play truant. I simply couldn't face going into school some mornings'

Who would have thought it? The boy who was once former Everton and Wales captain Kevin Ratcliffe's paper boy would go on to make his own headlines. Safe to say that in Kevin's eyes I was always a better footballer than I was a newspaper delivery boy because he never once gave me a tip at Christmas.

Amazingly, we were brought up on the same humble, working-class estate of Aston Park, Queensferry, North Wales.

My dad Roger had actually been born the other side of the England-Wales border, within the city walls of Chester. He was a decent footballer and even had trials at Wolves and played for Wrexham reserves but his father, my granddad Gerald, ended any ambitions he may have had of enjoying a career in the game. My granddad insisted that my dad learned a trade. Going into football in those days was far more risky than it is now and certainly didn't offer the current financial rewards.

Instead of kicking a ball for money he became a fitter and got himself a job making tow bars at a factory just along the canal in Chester. He then moved to the car production line at Vauxhall just a few miles away near Ellesmere Port. He was really pressurised to forget about a football career as my granddad worried about his ability to look after a young family which was soon to include me and my sister Lesley, plus my mum Carol.

Maybe the fact he couldn't become a professional footballer has helped me in some respects. My dad has always supported me and backed me in every way he could since I showed promise while kicking a ball about as a toddler. Perhaps he has lived the football dream through me, something I will always be grateful for. Even though he had a trade, times were hard, especially when the strikes hit the car industry as part of the years of industrial unrest in the early Seventies. He was forced to leave there and managed to get a job at a chemical works just down the road at Capenhurst.

By then, myself and my elder sister had arrived and we were living in Queensferry, having been born a few miles into Wales – something I am proud of and which was to give me many happy days as a footballer representing the country. There was never much money in those early days in Queensferry. In fact we were skint but neither Lesley or I were really aware of that because there was always food on the table. We didn't really want for anything, not that we ever asked. It was a loving home and that more than compensated for the lack of money as far as we were concerned. We didn't have lavish holidays, although when we were a little older my dad managed to purchase a modest caravan. So we would shoot off to places on the Wales coast like Abersoch and Tenby. It was a really enjoyable upbringing and helps put life into perspective. You don't need expensive gadgets or toys to be happy.

My dad still managed to play some football even if it was for the fun of it rather than seeing it pay the bills. He turned out for a local league side in Chester called Reliance who used to win everything. It wasn't the worst standard of football either. They were in the West Cheshire League. Sadly, he stopped playing when I was still fairly young. He had cartilage problems in both knees and while now you could probably be out walking on the same day as the operation, then it was virtually the end. The fact he had trouble in both knees was too much.

With four mouths to feed and money tight, my mum worked as well when she wasn't looking after Lesley or me. She was a hairdresser by trade but she would turn her hand to anything and had a number of other jobs to assist the finances.

We lived in a three-bedroom semi-detached house on Aston Park. In fact, my mum and dad still live there now. I still regard it as home. It wasn't and still isn't the most palatial area but I had many enjoyable years there. As long as there were lads the same age to kick a ball around with you were happy. I know times have changed and many parents would be panicking if it happened now but in the summer months, when I was eight or nine, I would be out until it got dark at 10pm. It's not as if my parents didn't know where I was. There was a park just 50 yards away so they knew I would be either playing football or cricket there.

A lot of those mates who used to enjoy a kickabout or hit a few sixes are still friends to this day. My best mate at the time, and he still is now, John Ratcliffe, is Kevin Ratcliffe's cousin. Having the same group of friends through the years helps keep you rounded as a person. If you ever dared step out of line, become too big for your boots, they would be there ready to knock you down a peg or two. It happens now. In many ways it's an extension of the football dressing room banter, which can often be cruel but is necessary to keep your feet firmly on the floor.

Obviously I still go back to Aston Park to visit my mum and dad. One day maybe I will be able to help them move to a nice bungalow somewhere, a place where they can really appreciate their retirement, but right now I know they are still content there. They have the same neighbours. The same people live opposite them. It's no problem when I turn up. Everyone knows who I am but hopefully I haven't changed too much from the football-mad kid who used to live there. I'm not into flash cars so it's not a great deal when I turn up. I would soon get some stick if the people there thought I had become Billy Big Time.

Football has, I suppose, been in my blood since around the age of six. But I wasn't too bad academically at first. I went to Queensferry Primary School and was pretty good at maths, geography and English. But I soon discovered that the best thing about the school was the fact Ron Bishop was in charge of the football there. If you know anything about the footballing backgrounds of players like Kevin Ratcliffe, Ian Rush, Michael Owen and Barry Horne, then the name Ron Bishop would no doubt have rung a few bells. I know all of them owe a huge debt of gratitude to Ron, who really fashioned their careers. I'm no different – it was a godsend as an impressionable, starry-eyed youngster to come under Ron's watchful and tutorial gaze. It amazes me how many professional players kicked their first ball in this small, unremarkable area just across the border from England.

At Queensferry Primary School there would be training under Ron's guidance virtually every night of the week. I'm certain in this day and age you wouldn't get that now. My dad was happy for me to become engrossed in the enjoyable training sessions put on by Ron. My dad, despite the fact he had played football at a decent standard, never pushed me, he just encouraged me to kick a ball from the time I was able to walk.

It's one of the most important things, not to be suffocated by pushy parents or a frenzied, egotistical teacher. I was left to enjoy what I was doing. Neither my dad or Ron were the pushy sort. My dad has never once told me to do this or do that and I think that sends out an important message to all parents. I've got kids of my own now and I watch them playing football, and I've got to say some parents and coaches are a real joke. I can honestly say my dad has never once raised his voice while watching me play as a youngster, he was always there to support me. It's dreadful what some parents get up to on the touchline, virtually going blue in the face blasting out orders. You can see the kids visibly cowering with fright. This doesn't do them any good whatsoever. I believe parents shouldn't be allowed to shout instructions from the side of the pitch.

It's interesting watching the Manchester United youngsters play. Even the coaches don't shout anything during the game. They let them play and offer their advice once the game is over. I've seen some kids who are very good playing but once they make a mistake they are petrified, expecting an immediate verbal volley from their watching parents or a blast from the coach. If the parents want their kids to be successful they must let them get on with it, not frightened of making mistakes along the way, which we all do.

It really winds me up what is happening now. Society has sadly changed in this respect and some of the dads who yell with veins coming out of their necks are real sad cases.

At the age of six, seven, I broke into my primary school football team and a year later I was also playing for the district side, Deeside Schools Under-11s. It wasn't because I was any bigger than the rest of the lads. If anything, at that age I was a little smaller. My biggest advantage was I was left-footed and so I was able to claim a place first as a left-back and then as a left-sided midfielder. Most of other lads were naturally right-footed.

Not that it started brilliantly. In my first game I scored an own goal and burst into tears. We were 1-0 down but luckily we went on to win 6-1, otherwise a career could have ended before it really got started.

In many ways I was three years ahead of the rest but it never fazed me playing against bigger kids. In fact, I was part of the Deeside team which went on win the Wales Under-11s Cup. We beat Cardiff in the semi-final and I remember how massive some of their players were. We then won against Swansea in the final, a team which included the former Wales international Chris Coleman, who must have been 6ft then!

Much of this enjoyment and success was down to Ron because he not only ran Queensferry Primary School Under-11s, he was also in charge of the Deeside team. It was due to him that I broke into the district side at such an early age. He obviously had great faith in me so I had been very fortunate to have gone to the right school, certainly regarding my footballing future. Ron was sport-mad. He wasn't married and all his spare time went into football coaching. I really looked up to him and I know that Ian Rush mentioned Ron in glowing terms in his autobiography.

There are a long line of players who are indebted to Ron. As I say, it's staggering to think just how many professional footballers have developed their skills on Deeside. Kevin Ratcliffe and I even came from the same street – two Wales captains who lived just a few houses from one another, how uncanny is that? Then there was Michael Owen – he was born in Chester – who has captained England and lived just half a mile away. I wouldn't get to know Kevin until a little later but I was well aware of him from an early age because his mum and dad still lived on our street.

The photos of Kevin and Rushy were amongst those plastered over the school walls, a constant reminder of what you were aspiring to be one day. I was one of those who would constantly gaze at the photos for inspiration. I thought if they can do it, why couldn't I?

With Ron Bishop around there was no better grounding if you wanted to try and make it as a footballer. He was so organised. We would walk onto the pitch in a line like you would see the football teams on the telly. We would have tracksuit tops on. Your boots had to be clean, your socks had to be up, never rolled down, and your shirt had to tucked inside your shorts.

When I played for the district side we would travel all around the country, Swansea, Newport, Cardiff. We would all cram into a minibus driven by Ron. My dad would watch most of my games and my mum Carol would also lend her support. It was a great football upbringing from an early age, a fantastic start for someone like myself who always wanted to become a professional footballer.

My one regret from that time was not continuing my cricket. I used to represent the Wales Under-11s side and really enjoyed the summer game, even though it only lasted a few months. We would play Middlesex, Essex, Hampshire, Kent and Surrey as we travelled all over the country. I remember playing against Mark Ramprakash. It was always second to football but I wished I could have played more. I love watching the game today.

My football suffered for a time when my primary schooldays ended. I started off at Deeside High School, which wasn't the best academically. I started to go off the rails, which meant that my studying was affected. It was quite a rough school and you had to be able to look after yourself. Inevitably, it was hard to keep out of scraps and it was too easy to become distracted from your school work. It was decided at the age of 13 that I should move schools. That was really down to my sister, who although she was decent at languages, failed one of her O-Levels. She wasn't able to resit it at Deeside so she moved to Hawarden High School where she could. With me having too many trips to see the headmaster for my parents' liking, they thought that Hawarden was the answer to my increasing disciplinary problems. The new school was undoubtedly better for my education but not really for my football.

It didn't keep me out of trouble either. In many ways the move made it worse on that front. I was forced to use my fists a bit because of the fact I had moved from a rival school and some of the Hawarden pupils were jealous of my football skills. That was when I was really glad to be mates with John Ratcliffe. I had got to know 'Basher' properly at Deeside High School. He was known as Basher because he used to knock other kids around, something which was to prove quite usual for me. He stood by me in my worst times when instead of going to school with a smile on my face, as had been the case, I felt really down in the dumps.

I would say the first couple of years there were the worst of my life. Kids can be cruel and I was left in no doubt from some of them about what they thought of me coming from the rival school. Eventually you are accepted but it got so bad sometimes that I would play truant. I simply couldn't face going into school some mornings.

The worst time was when my mum discovered what I had been up to. I had decided to go to the local park to kick a ball around instead of attending lessons. A sports teacher who wanted me to play football for the school team the next night rang my home and asked my mum whether I would be well enough to play. The game was up and when I came into the house she gave me a right telling off. She went absolutely berserk about me bunking off school.

I now knew I had to face my problems and not to run away. It was time to grow up. All this certainly toughened me up. What had been worse was I hadn't even been enjoying my football. In any case, football wasn't as important as it had been in my primary school days because at Hawarden it had to share the stage with rugby. My game also went off because I was growing, seemed to have less strength, and my confidence had suffered as a result. Even so I was still able to get into the Flintshire Under-13s representative side. We even reached the Welsh final, losing to Swansea.

By this time, mainly due to what I had achieved with the Deeside Under-11s, I had been making regular visits to Cheadle in Cheshire to train with a side attached to Manchester City. It was a nursery side and I had gone there like a flash after being spotted by a Manchester City scout. It was great because during school holidays you would go over to Manchester City for trials. At the time Andy Hinchcliffe, Paul Lake and David White were there. They were in the year above me while Jason Beckford, who went on to have a few games for the first team, was also in my year. Another team-mate was Chris Lightfoot, who later played for Chester City.

At the age of 13 I was told it was over – they didn't want me to come over anymore. And the man who made that decision, renowned City scout Ken Barnes, father of England international winger Peter, was the same person who told my dad – who was once on semi-pro terms at Wrexham – that he wasn't good enough and was being released. What a double family whammy! My dad was brilliant. Because he had the experience of it happening to him, he knew exactly how to handle my gut-churning knock-back. He advised me to keep going, to keep playing because I had lots of opportunities in front of me.

But despite his support there was no getting away from it, I was really upset. All this was further compounded by my failure to break into the Welsh Schoolboys side. I'm certain that was down to politics and not my ability. The guy who was in charge of the Wales-Under 15s at the time was from Wrexham. I played for Flintshire, who were Wrexham's big local rivals. While five or six of the Wrexham team got into the Wales side, just one was selected from Flintshire – and it wasn't me. The week after the Wales team was picked without me being selected, Flintshire played Wrexham and we beat them 3-0. I scored twice but it still wasn't enough for him to change his mind.

On reflection, knock-backs like this help you grow up. It's part of life and living but today we live in a cosseted world where kids are protected too much. We live in a society now that sneers at competition. We are very PC. Youngsters aren't allowed to be disappointed anymore. You can't upset them. They get to leave school having few experiences of any setbacks in their lives. When they start work they might walk straight into a rollicking but they can't handle it, after all they've had little experience. What are they going to do now, go home and cry to mum? Life is a competition when you go out there in the big wide world.

Sheffield United had also been interested in me and I spent a bit of time with them while the two local sides, Wrexham and Chester, had spotted me. I even went to Chester a few times, especially in the knowledge that Cliff Sear, who had started

Ian Rush on the road to fame and fortune by signing him for the Blues, had been instrumental in introducing me to the same club.

That all ended though when on the way back from having a trial with Sheffield United I took a call from another coach at Chester, Mick Buxton. He wanted me to play that afternoon but I said I couldn't because I'd already played that morning. He simply told me not to ever bother coming back to Chester. It was another blow, especially with Cliff being a great bloke. A few years later I bumped into Cliff and he asked why had I left Chester? I explained what had happened and he shook his head in disbelief.

Continuing to play for Flintshire, I was spotted at the age of 14, 15, by a Leeds United scout, Adrian Jones. He approached my teacher Steve Ellis and it was agreed that I would go to Leeds in the school holidays. When the time came around I was really nervous, especially after what had happened at Manchester City. At the same time I was definitely up for it. I'd had a few knock-backs, I didn't want any more.

My dad drove me over to Yorkshire and when you are coming down the motorway the huge city comes into view below you, along with Elland Road. It's an intimidating sight. I also felt uncomfortable when my dad dropped me off. Just off the motorway we had seen stacks of houses which appeared like rabbit hutches. One of them was to serve as my digs. I was scared when my dad departed having handed me a £10 note for my spends.

At least it was comforting to know I wasn't alone in the digs because there was another Welsh lad, a Leeds apprentice,

Lyndon Simmonds staying there. He tried to make it as comfortable as it could be for me.

The next day wasn't the greatest start to life at Leeds. I knew I had to catch a bus to Elland Road, which I did, no problem. But I suddenly realised the only cash I had was the £10 note donated by my dad. The fare was 10p. The driver went absolutely ballistic. What a welcome to the big city. I was almost sick with fear. I felt so vulnerable but there was also the excitement of what lay ahead once I got off the ruddy bus.

Luckily, Pete Gunby, the Leeds United youth team coach, was a nice bloke and tried to make me feel at home. Even so, at first you still had to fend for yourself. After all, I was just a trialist hoping to make an impact, so it was a case of get your own kit, get changed and show what you can do. Thankfully I was able to do just that.

I seemed to have come a long way since receiving stick from Kevin Ratcliffe over the late delivery of his morning paper. My paper round was around an estate in Shotton, Deeside, near my home.

Kevin lived on a hill overlooking it, in a more upmarket area. His was always the last paper I delivered and if I got a puncture and I was looking to be late for school he'd had it, I wouldn't bother going to his house. The number of rollickings he used to give me because he couldn't take his newspaper with him to training at Everton! As a result he never gave me a tip at Christmas. Even though he knew I was his cousin's best mate it didn't make any difference. He would give me a real earful. We have a laugh about it now. I tell him I'm still waiting for those tips!

The best tips were the ones he gave on the football field because occasionally he would join Basher, me and some other kids for a kickabout on the local playing field. What an experience that was, playing football with the Everton and Wales captain.

2

Louise's story

HOW WE FELL IN LOVE

'He turned up at my 13th birthday party and I wondered what he was doing there because he hadn't been invited. It was a house party for my friends. It was supposed to be fancy dress, not that the boys bothered. Obviously Gary just thought he could come along with the lads who had received invites'

G ary and I met at Hawarden High School. We were both in the third year. But to be perfectly honest, although most of the girls fancied him because he was a good-looking lad, I didn't! I had a boyfriend at the time so I wasn't that interested.

He turned up at my 13th birthday party and wondered what he was doing there because he hadn't been invited. It was a house party for my friends. It was supposed to be fancy dress, not that the boys bothered. Thankfully the girls did. Obviously

39

Gary just thought he could come along with the lads who had received invites.

During the party was the first time I had really spoken to him and I was attracted to his humour. He made me laugh.

Later one evening I was playing tennis and he was playing football with some lads on the pitch by the side of the tennis courts. Maybe he was attracted to my tennis skills, I'm not sure. But at school the next day he asked one of the girls – he was too shy to ask me himself – whether I would go out with him. I said no. I still didn't really know him.

He didn't give up. He asked a second girl to ask me again and back went the same answer. Then came a telephone call from one of his friends but I hadn't changed my mind. A third girl on his behalf then wondered whether I would like to play tennis with him? I thought that was okay – I didn't mind playing tennis with him.

So on a nice June evening I went along to Hawarden Park as arranged, dressed in all my tennis gear complete with racket. There waiting for me was Gary on his bike – and it quickly became obvious he didn't have any intent to play tennis. He didn't have a racket. In the end it didn't matter because we got on really well that evening, chatting on about lots of things.

Even at that age he was talking about what he wanted to do in the future – that he didn't want to bring children up in certain areas. He talked about where he would love to have a house where he could fish, with a river nearby, things like that. Where we ended up living in our house in Chester, it did have a lake at the back where he could fish. He already had his dream set, even at that young age.

We then started going out together, although many of the dates were just wandering around Hawarden Park chatting away or watching TV at home. We walked his nan's dog and enjoyed the odd trip to the cinema. We couldn't afford to do much else.

Gary was well into his football and during school holidays he would go off to different places. He did his O-Levels when the World Cup was on, which wasn't the best because I'm sure it affected his studying, but even so he came out with six or seven without really trying. He was a clever boy really even though football was his main thing.

How good a footballer he was didn't really bother me. I knew he was very passionate about football but I never went to see him play at that age. It wasn't until he went up to Leeds United that I would watch him, travelling to games with his mum and dad, Roger and Carol. Going to Leeds was a big test for the relationship but it held up well.

I had been sporty myself. I was the under-16 badminton champion for the county, loved playing tennis and other sports, but I didn't really do anything with the talent I must have had. I suppose no-one pushed me. I still love my sport and have since run two marathons. I think that helped bring us closer together – a mutual love of always trying to be active and to stay fit.

As far as badminton was concerned I got a bit bored with it and was just ready to move onto something else. Maybe I regret that now, looking back, not having pursued the badminton. I think I should have progressed with some of the sports but when I started work it was a case of concentrating more on fitness lessons. I started doing A-Levels for a short time before deciding I wanted a job. I wanted to earn some money.

During those times you could go out and get a job if you really wanted one. So that's what I did because Gary had gone on to join Leeds as a YTS youngster.

I was the one with the job and the spending money for whenever he went out. I had managed to get taken on by the Midland Bank in Buckley, North Wales. So I was the main earner. Gary would come back home on the coach to see me at weekends. He couldn't afford a car and so he had to use public transport.

He was living in a council house area of Seacroft, near Leeds. I never really fancied going to the house he was living in if I'm honest. But I did go there once and met Alan and Margaret, who were his landlords. I sat there in a sea of cigarette smoke – a long way from what today's young players will experience. It wasn't an easy time for Gary. He often said that at times he had felt homesick.

To try to help we would write letters to one another. I know he really looked forward to seeing what I had written to him. In fact, I've still got those letters. There were no mobile phones then so you couldn't text one another, so the best way of keeping in touch was by sending letters.

I looked through some of his letters he had written to me in his early days at Leeds around two years after his death.

37 KENTMERE AVENUE
SEACROFT,
LEEDS
LS14 6QD.
TEL 0532 - 733113.

Dear Louise,

This is my second day at Leeds, and my first day's training was today. It was boiling hot and we trained for four hours solid, and I lost over half a stone in weight.

My digs are in a place called Seacroft which is one of the roughest areas in Leeds. I am staying in a large council house with a few other lads and the family. When I first saw the house ● I thought I would hate it, but suprisingly I am settling in great and getting on well with everyone.

I am writing this while you are still on holiday, but I am thinking about you all the time so I had to write, although knowing that you won't recieve the letter until

you get back. Don't forget to ring my Dad when you come home, so that you can come to the Airport and pick us up. Love you and always thinking about you,

lots of love
Gary
xxx

There was another letter I discovered – reproduced at the start of the book – which read as follows:

Dear Louise,

I don't really know what to say. I have been thinking about finishing at Leeds, I've also been thinking of other things which I won't say. I'm so depressed. I'm just going to go to sleep now and hope I never wake up. I love you so much, I will always love you.

I don't know what else to say except you might see me sooner than you think, or otherwise. You never leave my mind, nothing else seems to matter anymore. I love you more than you can imagine.

Gary
xxx

Considering what eventually happened to him, this letter really stood out – as anyone reading it now can see. When I found it, this letter didn't have a stamp on the envelope so I don't know if Gary actually posted it. Or it could have been with another one in which he told me not to take any notice of this letter. But you can tell that he was very dependent on my letters.

Maybe something had happened early on which he had kept to himself? I would cheer him up with different things and the letters would go backwards and forwards between us. It was lovely. He would always look forward to my letters.

I can't remember reading this particular letter at the time at all. Or maybe I knew I was seeing him very soon after it arrived, so I could have been thinking 'how ridiculous' or whatever, I honestly don't know. Maybe as a 17-year-old I hadn't really taken on board any deeper meaning in the letter.

But re-reading it, the letter seems to say it all really when you consider how he ended his life. If he had a mental illness then he probably had it from an early age. Maybe Gary was a timebomb waiting to explode at some point.

Looking at his letter now is like a lightbulb moment in many ways. It answers an awful lot about why he did what he did. Maybe the mental illness or depression, however you want to describe it, was always there from an early age and returned at times in his later life. It seems that no-one knew what was going on in his head at times.

The letter when you go over it again is very succinct – it says a lot in not so many words. "I'm just going to go to sleep now and I hope I never wake up" is not something a normal 16-year-old or 17-year-old would write, is it? Or not a well one.

These letters showed that at the time I was his world. The only reason he was up in Leeds was for our life later on. They show how he dreamt of a nice home, of this, that and the other. How he was prepared to make sacrifices for the dreams to come true. In many ways he was old before his time.

I think he was so impressed with my letter-writing he suggested in one of his that I should write a book. This time apart proved we were in love. It was also healthy to have some distance between us because he could do some of his growing up in Leeds while I could do the things I wanted back home in North Wales. Some people back home were getting married at 18,19, but we didn't really want that so in many ways it was probably good he had moved away.

He broke into the Leeds first team when he was 18 and I would watch some of the games with Roger and Carol. Carol would make some sandwiches and bring a flask of something hot to enjoy on the journey. It was a nice day out and for me it wasn't really about watching Gary play football, it was more about seeing him again and spending time with him. The football for me was secondary.

I was proud of him and what he was achieving at a young age. I am probably more proud now when I reflect on all that and having my own two sons, Ed and Tommy.

It was fantastic when Leeds won the First Division championship in 1992. It was also the time when we decided I should move to Yorkshire to join Gary. It had been make-or-break for us on a personal level due to it being a long-distance relationship. It meant me having to give up my job, which was a blow. I tried to get a transfer to another bank in the Leeds area but there was nothing available.

I still wanted to do something and so I started working in a shop called Accent which was owned by a friend of Gary's. I enjoyed it because I helped with the window displays and then helped out on the buying front. I felt I had realised my vocation – this was me. I had always wanted to venture into the world of shops, retail. My parents thought, no, go to work in a bank because I would qualify for a cheaper mortgage or be able to get a cheaper car loan. I knew where they were coming from. Banking wasn't what I wanted, long term. I couldn't add up for a start, if I'm being honest!

Our first place together was in Leeds city centre. Gary was renting an apartment. It was great for me because I could just walk up the main street to my work. It was perfect. A few months later we bought our first house in a nice area close to Wetherby. He was ready to invest in somewhere, having put some money to one side.

Although Leeds had won the championship, I hadn't really been part of the celebrations because I was working and couldn't always get any time off. So I felt a little detached from all that really. I knew though that Gary was starting to make a name for himself. I'd become friendly with some of the Leeds players and their wives. There was David and Mandy Batty, Gary and Denise McAllister, Chris and Amanda Fairclough, David and Leanne White, Rod and Rachael Wallace, Gordon and Lesley Strachan.

There was Lee Chapman and Leslie Ash, not that we were really close. I just remember looking up to Leslie and wanting to be like her. She was everyone a girl could wish to be. I was just completely awestruck. More so with her and what she represented than the football.

I think after a time at Leeds I realised I had found myself more. It had been good moving away from home and being with Gary. I think with me there he had reined himself in a bit. He had been going out a lot and now it was a more stable environment and I think he appreciated that. We didn't know how the relationship was going to go, being together.

It proved to be very enjoyable. We would go out a lot with Gary's agent at the time, Hayden Evans, and his wife Jean. They didn't live too far away. Often a big gang of us would go out, which was great.

We knew our relationship was going to go one way or the other. Thankfully everything was positive.

On the football side everything was moving in the right direction under the manager Howard Wilkinson, who Gary had great respect for.

It moved on for us as well when Gary proposed marriage. He came back from taking part in a photoshoot for one of the lads' mags, *Nuts* or *Loaded*. He said he had been thinking about getting engaged. There wasn't any grand statement. We both agreed that, yes it would be nice to eventually get married. Everything felt right. I think for me it made me feel more complete, more confident about things. It means you can start moving forward and planning for the future.

The next step was also probably to have children and we felt for both our parents' sakes to do it in wedlock. I suppose nowadays it's quite normal to have your children in your wedding pictures.

We got married locally at Hawarden Church. It was a lovely sunny day. The night before, Gary had stayed at his best man's house while I had been at my mum's. I remember her bringing me cornflakes in the morning, complete with warm milk! I was very excited. It turned out to be a dream day helped by the gorgeous weather. After the wedding ceremony we went off to the Grosvenor Hotel in Chester for our reception. We also stayed the night there. I love the hotel and we've had one of the boy's christenings there. It meant a lot to us.

Gary was also in the process of moving clubs for the first time, with Everton ready to sign him. As we approached the red carpet going into the Grosvenor, someone shouted something like "great move to Everton" to Gary, which was lovely.

Our honeymoon was a tour of California ending up in Hawaii. It was in Hawaii that Gary received a phone call to confirm that Everton had agreed a fee with Leeds to buy him and he could travel to Everton for a medical when we arrived back in England. He'd been at Leeds around 10 years and so it seemed a natural time for Gary to move on. He was really excited about the move because Everton was the team he had supported as a boy.

So soon after we landed back in England, Gary grabbed his toilet bag and shot off for his medical at Everton.

Now of course he is back in the North West while I'm up in Yorkshire – signs of times to come as part of the hectic life of a footballer. I eventually followed him and we rented a property in Marford, back in North Wales. It was great we were back on home soil and, even better, Ed was on his way as our first child and a planned honeymoon baby.

It all seemed so close-knit again being on familiar territory with our parents close at hand. We were also back amongst old friends.

3

Friends' story

IN A BAD PLACE

Kevin Ratcliffe

*Grew up on the same street as Gary, and
played alongside him for Wales*

I was in the press room at the Liberty Stadium with my lad Dean and due to cover Swansea's Premier League game with Aston Villa for Irish radio. Suddenly, someone wanted a word with me outside the room. I honestly can't remember who it was because even now it seems so surreal. "What's the problem?" I asked. Back came the reply that Gary Speed had died – that he had committed suicide. I just fell back against the wall and felt absolutely shit.

I went back into the room and told Dean, who like me could hardly believe it.

The radio station offered me the chance of pulling out of my commitment because they could gather how upset I was at hearing the news. But I wanted to carry on. To be perfectly honest I was a little surprised the game went ahead, especially with it being in Wales and Gary being manager of the country.

It was particularly hard on Shay Given, who of course was due to play for Aston Villa that afternoon. He was very good friends with Gary, having got to know him well during their days at Newcastle together. It hurt me to see how obviously it was hurting him. He's about to play a game and he's breaking down in floods of tears.

It must have been so difficult but I suppose we are professionals and the show has to go on. Somehow you just have to switch into your professional mode.

I'm glad my son was with me so that I didn't have to travel back in the car on my own. But it didn't stop the long moments of silence as all kinds of emotions went through my head. Why Gary? What has happened? What the hell has gone on?

I spoke to my cousin John [Basher], who was very close to Gary. He had been to the Speeds' house that morning after hearing the tragic news. He was at the house when I phoned him and he walked outside to take my call. He had earlier been phoned by Gary's wife Louise. Now he was yelling down the phone to me: "What's gone on? Why has he done it?" He was fuming, really fuming about Gary doing this – and for what?

But Gary must have been in a bad place. Immediately on hearing the news you don't think about that. You look at him leaving a young family behind, his wife would be in bits. I thought, 'Gary, you're selfish – there's your parents, your sister.

You've left behind an almighty mess and they have got to pick up the pieces.'

Then, of course, they will all eventually want to know why. And that is true to this day. We will never know. A part of me still thinks he was very selfish and couldn't deal with whatever problem he had. Then another part of me thinks, was it an illness?

Was it something we couldn't detect? You can usually see, for instance, when people have been drinking heavily or have gambling problems. You accept those are illnesses and need curing. But with depression you can't always see that in a person. You don't really know what they are thinking or what they are going through.

Gary had been on BBC TV's Football Focus the day before he had hanged himself. I had played golf with him the week before. Everything seemed in order. The biggest thing that bugs me to this day, and I know it's the same for my cousin as well, is if you had a problem Gary, why didn't you speak to us?

After all, I'd known him since he was a young kid – since he was my paper boy. Why hadn't he asked to have a word with me? But as a professional footballer you often keep many things to yourself. As a manager, which he was, everyone comes to you with their problems. You deal with them. Maybe he got to a point where he couldn't deal with his own problems. I don't know.

As I mentioned, we were playing golf at Frodsham, near Chester. There was me, Basher and David Johnson, the former Liverpool and Everton player. Why didn't he take one of us to one side and mention what may have been worrying him? He never mentioned a single thing.

Around four or five days later, he had gone somewhere abroad and Sky Sports were covering the event. I was watching the TV with my wife Sharon. The pictures showed Gary walking from his taxi and Sharon immediately said to me: "Oh, what's wrong with Gary?" She said that he didn't look right – and that has sat with me over the years.

For her it was something she had picked out in his looks and features. She had certainly seen something I hadn't noticed.

Talking of his looks – he could easily have been a male model, a film star. You certainly didn't want to be anywhere near him in a photo. But that's the outside. Who knows what was going on inside his head?

Maybe that tells you there is an illness somewhere because when you think you have got everything, a nice family, a nice house, it doesn't mean you do really have everything. In Gary's case, with what happened, it all points to an illness. But how do you spot that? Nobody is really trained in that way. Ideally you would want a spotter – someone in football who can see the early signs maybe of depression, someone who might be able to offer advice and try and nip it in the bud.

Because of what happened to Gary, I look at football managers in a different way now. You can see the pressure they put on themselves. It's there in their faces. I think to myself now, 'He's aged or he looks ill.' I can see the strain.

With Gary it took him time to take you into his trust, which again was probably a sign that he was a deep thinker.

The family, of course, were absolutely devastated at his death. His mother Carol said at the inquest that Gary was someone who looked at his glass half empty rather than half full. It must be very hard for a mother not to get a real answer about why the tragedy happened. You never get over something like that.

I'd known him growing up. As a paper boy he used to moan that I never gave him a tip at Christmas. No wonder – I never used to get my paper until after 9am! He was still at school then so obviously he wasn't getting into school until late. I think I was the last one on his round. In the end I stopped having it delivered because I was leaving for training at Everton without seeing it.

He was 13,14 then. He grew up with my cousin John. He would often pop round with John, asking for tickets for Everton games. Quite often I would join them, even though I was playing for Everton, and some of their mates for a kickaround on a field just down the road. The three of us were all left footers. I didn't realise how good a footballer Gary was, even though he played for the local schools sides. I then heard he was signing for Leeds United. I thought to myself, why Leeds? Why not go to a local club like Everton, Liverpool or Manchester United?

After that, when he came down for a kickabout I took more notice and could see that everything in the game was so easy for him, his touch, his passing. After becoming an apprentice at Leeds he would come back to Everton at times to watch me play. He came into the players' lounge on a couple of occasions. We then bought Ian Snodin from Leeds and Gary had been Snod's boot boy, cleaning his boots as part of his duties. I hope he was a better boot boy than paper boy!

His mum and dad still live on the same street as mine. My mum and dad have been there now 50-odd years. That's why I've always had an affinity with him, which carried on when he broke into the Wales squad, even though there's almost a 10-year age gap. I've also played against him on a few occasions when he was at Leeds.

He won the First Division title, the last season before the Premier League started, with Leeds. Despite only being a young kid he did fantastically well for them. He was exceptional in the air – he was brave. He played wide on the left when they won the title. It was only in his later years that he moved into central midfield. It was a great start to his career. To get a medal at that age and to play in so many games was exceptional.

I think he used to room with Gordon Strachan because he would tell me what a fitness fanatic Gordon was and how he would eat the right things, like bananas. It's one of the main reasons why Gary played on well into his thirties because through Gordon he learned to look after himself. He also picked up international experience at a young age with Wales and would look at the older pros like myself. You could see he wanted to learn and better himself.

He was always a very personable lad who never forgot his roots. He still played golf at his local club and joined in the quiz nights at the pub whenever he was around in the area, drinking glasses of orange. He still liked the home comforts.

He loved his two sons, Eddie and Tommy, and that's one of the main reasons why his death is hard to take. That's also why I'm pretty sure he had an illness. For you to go down that road means there is something drastically wrong inside you. Something triggered it.

It's still hard to take. If we had lost him in a car crash then it's more acceptable. People talk about depression a lot but where are the signs in someone? Did Louise see anything? A suicide always leaves a host of unanswered questions. The family has to move on because you can't think he is going to walk back through the door.

Howard Wilkinson

Managed Gary at Leeds, where he was part of the team that won the First Division title in 1992

I was in Majorca with my wife Sam. It was our traditional 10-day trip before the hectic Christmas build-up.

It was a Sunday morning and I was looking out over a golf course and the sea, and by normal standards it wasn't the nicest of days. It was about to get a lot worse. I got that dreadful phone call from Gordon Strachan.

Gordon opened up the conversation by saying: "Have you heard?" There was a pause and then he went on: "Gary's died?" "Gary who?" I replied. "Gary," said Strach. "Speedo."

My first thought was he had been involved in an accident. I don't think at that point it had really sunk in. How it had happened was still very confusing but no matter how it had occurred, one thing was horribly clear – he was dead. I was surprised, shocked, stunned – it was hard, almost impossible, to take in.

I can't say I spoke to him every week after he left Leeds United but we chatted more regularly when he joined Sheffield United towards the end of his playing career. I'd often seen him on telly and he had never looked any different to the

Gary Speed I knew. I'd got to know his dad Roger very well, which impacted even more because of the unimaginable hurt the family would be going through. He'd first asked to see me when Gary was coming through at Leeds. He wanted to thank me for what he felt I'd done for his son.

I'd treated Gary similarly to some of the other younger players I encountered like Harry Kewell, Jonathan Woodgate, Paul Robinson, Gary Kelly and David Batty – all the kids I had introduced. I tried to look after them. Gary hadn't settled straightaway but with others, David Batty for instance, it didn't matter where he was, he was no different, whether he was playing in a game at Wembley or at Accrington Stanley. Gary was less assured, a bit shy.

When he did get into the first team he teamed up with Batts off the field and I had to have words with them on a few occasions. They were just being lads but at times they needed to be told, telling them about the long term and how far they might progress in the game.

I think Roger had appreciated that. But the one thing from an early age was when Gary trained, he really did train, even before older players like Gordon Strachan came in to help influence him. He was serious about his football. He could see it had to be worked at, that it was a profession.

I told him I felt he had the capacity to play well into his thirties, the way he was working – that he understood the benefits of the work he was doing. If he ate right etc, he would have a long career. I also told him that one day he would make a good captain.

He giggled at that – the little laugh which was never far away. I explained that teams didn't always have to be led by players who bawl and shout like Terry Butcher, Tony Adams and so on. Sometimes captains are captains by example, by the way they go about things. How they are viewed by other people, how they are respected. It's about the message. Postmen don't have to shout all the time, it's about delivering. If you want to talk the talk, you have to walk the walk.

Some people are ready for captaincy when they are 21, 22. Others grow into it because it takes time to develop the necessary character.

I'd first come across Gary on the day of my first game at Elland Road as Leeds United manager. I went early to watch the Under-18s play at the training ground. I stood next to the youth coach Peter Gumby. I'm sure Gary was playing left-back that day. I asked Peter to talk me through the team and when we got to Gary he said that this lad had a chance. He added that he was a wide-left player.

From my point of view, the qualities I first saw in him were character, application, left sided and good in the air. Ultimately, he displayed all that by the time we both left Leeds. And by that time for different reasons he had also played in every position except in goal.

When you make positional changes you have got to know that person. Move some people to a position they are not familiar with and it worsens the team because the player sulks. You learn not to do it. But with Gary, if the game demanded it, he just went and played there and he would try his best to do whatever was needed. Technically, he was invaluable.

He was good in the air, so invaluable at set-pieces either against you or for you. He was a bonus in those situations. He had a great engine, getting up and down the pitch. A good left foot, was adaptable. He could defend as well as he attacked. To have a player like that was an incredible weapon. He would also weigh in with eight, nine, 10 goals in a season, which was also a huge benefit.

He probably came of age away at Southampton in our first season in Division One after gaining promotion. He scored early on from outside the box, a real player's goal. He controlled and despatched it brilliantly. That night I thought he had emerged. Like a butterfly, he had emerged from the cocoon. I thought to myself that he would fly now – and he did.

He would join Batty, Strachan and Gary McAllister in the side – they were a fantastic quartet. I'd got Strachan early on before we were promoted. You see someone when they are playing against you but when they are training with you, you see even more, and with Strach I saw a versatility. I saw a versatility in Gary. When I brought in Gary McAllister it was at the cost of Vinnie Jones [now a Hollywood actor] and I've told Vinnie since that I should have kept him.

Vinnie had a heart as big as a house. He was very generous, he was a team man. In a different way to Gordon Strachan, he was a leader. I said to him the last time we were together that if I'd have kept him – which I should have done – just for the example he had set, he would have been a manager by now. He replied: "Well thank god you didn't because I'm a lot richer now than if I had gone into football management!"

But once McAllister came in we had two, three, four ways of approaching a game. One which we used a lot away from home was Rod Wallace, wide left, Strachan on the right, Lee Chapman in the middle. Gary would then be a third midfielder

with Batty and McAllister. We could change it and push Rod
in alongside Chappy, which would mean Gary going out wide
to the left, making it a 4-4-2, or change it by pushing Rod in,
keeping Gary inside alongside Batty, Strachan and McAllister,
giving space for our full-backs to attack.

Having so many ways of playing worked for us. In our first
season in Division One we finished fourth and the next season
we added McAllister with the initial aim of collecting one more
point than the previous season. Only then would we look at
the bigger picture. Before every season I would sit down with
the players and agree what we could realistically achieve.

We knew that if we realised the target then we wouldn't be
too far away from being contenders to win the league. We
ended up achieving that and for Gary it was the season he
really took off. His form was such that he could have got into
any of the British national sides, not just Wales. As far as a
manager is concerned he was everything you wanted – high
performance and low maintenance.

People assume Eric Cantona, who we brought to the
club in the February of the title-winning season, was high
maintenance. He wasn't. He came in because Chapman got
injured at Tottenham. We were told that it was him finished
for the season after picking up a horrendous facial injury. The
surgeon had told us that he would possibly need a skin graft.

Cantona had gone walkabout again at his club. I think he
had, shall we say, strong words with the club president. He
had definitely fallen out with people at Monaco. I'd seen him
before playing for France Under-21s and knew he was very
good.

I rang Gerard Houllier, Michel Platini and Glenn Hoddle

about Eric. They all said the same thing – he was a very good player but a... I think he'd had about 10 clubs when I got him.

Back to Chappy. After seeing him I rang Brendan Ingle, the boxing trainer, who knew a thing about facial cuts. I asked him if he could do me a favour and look at fixing Chappy so that he could play a lot quicker than forecast. He told me about a special healing solution he used on his boxers so Chappy was told to bathe his face with this stuff almost every hour. It worked and he was back much quicker.

However, I'd brought in Eric and he ended up starting seven games and scoring three goals, which obviously helped us win the league.

But for whatever reason, what we had in the title-winning season disappeared during the following campaign. We couldn't win away from home.

We went out of the Champions League, our workrate dropped, our organisation was less tight. I left Eric out. I had told him on the Saturday morning but by the time we were due to meet for lunch he'd disappeared. Gary McAllister told me: "Boss, he's gone. He's left."

I can't pay Gary Speed a bigger accolade than saying he was our player of the season in the year we won the league. It was a close call but during the campaign, in addition to his goals, he was always prepared to do some of the less fashionable jobs on behalf of the team.

Gordon could do what Gordon could do, Gary Mac could do what Gary Mac could do, Chappy could do what Chappy could do. You could say that about all of them, but Gary could do you a job anywhere. One day he played at centre-half.

I know that Gary became very influenced by Strach's lifestyle.

When I went for Gordon it looked like he was going to Sheffield Wednesday. At the time they were in Division One, we were in Division Two. I pleaded with him to come to Leeds for a chat. I talked him through what our plans. Gordon felt his career was on a downward spiral because of his age and his later performances at Manchester United – the fact that Alex [Ferguson] was prepared to let him go.

He felt he was in the twilight of his career. But I took him through our five-year plan which would hopefully enable us to compete for the First Division title. I outlined the crucial part he could play. I convinced him that when you get older you don't train less, but you train much smarter. I told him I was looking for leadership, someone who could be a role model for the diets I was encouraging.

The first thing I did when I joined Leeds was go into the kitchen. At the time they were one of the first clubs to actually serve meals for the players. Don Revie had started it. I asked to see a menu, then introduced a healthier, more athlete-appropriate diet.

Gordon had been turned on by all this because by then he already enjoyed a healthy-eating regime which involved lots of bananas, for instance, after seeing what benefits tennis players enjoyed from eating them at the side of the court.

At Notts County and Sheffield Wednesday, I had started talking to specialists about fitness and lifestyle. It became obvious to me, for example, that players dehydrate at different rates. You see some players who have run their socks off yet their shirts are dry, while others who haven't run so much are soaked. We ended up with rehydration drinks which suited individual players' needs.

All that helped convince Gordon to join us. And pretty soon he realised that he wasn't just going to be a bit-player in our plans, but would play a major part. He also understood the tactical side so he could help me with any changes on the field.

Both he and Gary Mac have since said to me they hadn't believed at first that I could make them fitter. Both said it was a load of rubbish when people claim you can't get fitter once you reach the age of 30.

In certain senses, Gordon was fitter than he had been as a young player at Aberdeen. Gary took note of all this as a young player at Leeds and replicated this when he moved onto the likes of Everton and Newcastle. In his later years, kids would look at him and see how he prepared.

Even when he was finishing as a player at Sheffield United, his preparations for a game were no less excellent than at anywhere else. He also told me when I met him a few years ago that he had taken up yoga and pilates. It's easy to make a body fit but to keep it fit there has to be a fit man with a fit brain. He learned that lesson early on and saw an example of it in Gordon. Gary absorbed all the good things he saw going on around him.

Career-wise, he had everything in front of him. It's all hard to understand but something that Vinnie Jones once told me has stayed with me and is important when you consider what happened to Gary. I was expressing my disbelief, how can anybody do that? Vinnie then disclosed he had once been on the verge of doing the same thing. An inexplicable dark moment he did not see coming.

Sometimes you don't know about how people can slip into dark moods. Vinnie had also told me that he was devastated when I sold him to Sheffield United. I had never realised that.

But from the work we do with the League Managers Association, such problems are not as rare as one might think. I made it my business to talk to some of the experts in this field that we employ. They gave me the figure of unexplained suicides. It's frightening.

It's a huge loss. You cannot begin to comprehend the impact this had on his wife Louise, the boys, his parents and sister. In a totally different way, the loss also impacted greatly on the game. He had become a huge positive influence on the game and people in it. There would be players and people around now who would have been better for his presence.

Simon Grayson

Rose up the junior ranks alongside Gary, and they remained in touch throughout their careers

I was manager of Leeds United and at the training ground at Thorpe Park preparing for a game at Nottingham Forest which was coming up on the Tuesday night. I got a call from our physio, Alan Sutton, with the terrible news of what had happened earlier that morning with Gary. I immediately switched on Sky Sports and there was confirmation of something I could scarcely believe. Like everybody, I was just stunned, shocked, because no-one who really knew him could have foreseen this.

He appeared to be enjoying what he was doing with Wales

as their manager. He had just been on Football Focus the day before. It sent my head into a spin. No way could I have ever envisaged being confronted with this awful news. Glynn Snodin, who was my assistant manager at Elland Road, also knew Gary well because the three of us had been together as youngsters at Leeds in the late 1980s, early '90s. We just looked at each other that Sunday morning in disbelief and completely heartbroken.

I ended up sitting in the office while others on the staff took training. I continued to watch the telly for any more news, almost in a daze. The whole day was just surreal, one you wish had never happened. I was alone trying to take everything in.

We were the same age, with hopefully so much in front of us. Everything on the surface appeared fine with Gary, his home life with Louise and the boys, and he was in charge of his national side. My first thoughts were with the family and I was unable to imagine what they were going through that morning. The whole football world was in a state of shock.

At the age of 14 we had both signed associated schoolboy forms for Leeds United. I went to Elland Road to watch a match with my parents and before the game we went into a room to sign the forms – and there doing the same was Gary with his mum and dad.

The first thing I remember was Gary's Welsh accent. Coming from North Yorkshire, this was the first time I'd ever heard this accent. I thought, he doesn't sound like the rest of us, because most of the young players taking the first steps to become a professional footballer were from the Yorkshire area and all sounded the same. As soon as Gary spoke the complete difference hit me.

Between the ages of 14 and 16 we were at Leeds training camps together during school holidays. In our last year at school we started playing for the Under-18s side, or at least being around it, getting the odd game here and there. It was a good grounding for when we became full-time apprentices.

What was fantastic was the fact we were playing on pitches right next to Elland Road. It's now a car park but in our apprentice days you couldn't have a bigger incentive to try and make it, with the first-team ground just yards away.

The first team trained there as well and so you would often be on the next pitch to them, and seeing them at close quarters was inspirational. Being a Leeds fan made it even more special for me, while I know that Gary was a boyhood Evertonian.

We had all worked hard to get to where we were, striving to eventually break into the first-team squad. Gary had a fantastic left foot, appeared to have natural ability but still, like myself, wanted to work hard to develop, improve our game and iron out any weaknesses. He had non-stop energy and an incredible heading ability. His heading really stood out from an early age.

David Batty was a year older, although we ended up playing in the same junior sides as him. It was a great group of lads, complete with plenty of pranks.

We were also both in digs and Gary would always complain that I was in a lovely village in a five-bedroom house next to a pub. He was in Seacroft, which let's say wasn't as nice an environment. We both had to travel into training on a bus but I was constantly reminded that I had come up trumps with the selection of digs after both becoming apprentices.

We had a few good nights out together, although Gary was

more keen on them than me. I would often go home to see my parents, leaving him to it when he wasn't seeing his own parents. There were plenty of times when we went out as a group and got up to a few things. Gary would be very much at the heart of any mischief.

I can recall one of the players being tied to a lamppost, completely naked, being doused by a hose pipe. I don't think these days you would be able to get away with something like that. That was part of the initiation process any new young player would have to go through.

You could be in a room at the training ground, cleaning boots, when the door would suddenly close behind you. It would quickly be locked and the light would go off while some of the other lads would fling the boots around, leaving the unsuspecting victim with a few bruises. You just hoped if you got struck with a boot it had rubber soles rather than the big metal ones.

One of Gary's mates, Sam Jones, was one of the biggest pranksters. Being a Scouser and mad goalkeeper, you had to keep well clear of him. He didn't seem to be concerned about any consequences of his actions.

Billy Bremner was the manager and he was brilliant with the young players. I was entrusted with cleaning his boots and also with cleaning out the coaches' office. I would love hearing some of the stories that Billy and his coaches would tell while I was going about my chores.

Once the jobs had been completed, emptying the bins, cleaning the floors etc, and looking forward to going home, Billy would get out a football and tell myself and other apprentices who had completed their apprentice duties to join him in the car park for a kickabout. Sometimes we'd even play in the corridor area which we had just cleaned, which meant having to mop up again once Billy had finished. No one minded because it was a fantastic education for any young player.

Once we were taking part in a five-a-side game with Billy watching on in his suit. Within a few minutes he couldn't resist it anymore and he joined in the game still wearing his suit and ordinary shoes. We all loved it. He was so enthusiastic and you want to emulate someone like that. He wasn't adverse to making a few naughty tackles and we'd then do the same to try and impress him. He was a great motivator, an inspiration to the likes of Gary and myself.

It was sad to see him go. He had also given me my debut at the age of 17. I was the first one out of the group, which included Speedo, to make it into the senior side. There was no better feeling. I was the captain of the youth team at that time and Gary and I would play in central midfield together.

Although we were big mates, we knew that we were competing to be selected for the different sides, the Under-18s, the reserves and finally of course, the big one – the first team.

It was great to be picked for the first team from my perspective. But I think it was also good for Gary because it encouraged him to try and follow suit. It was healthy competition amongst us all because we all wanted to have successful careers as professional footballers.

My debut was away against Huddersfield – a classic 0-0! I had played on the Saturday for the Under-18s. I picked up a little knock but I felt I would be fine to train on the Monday. Someone said that there was a rumour going around that I might be training with the first team. It came true and the next evening I was making my first-team debut. But it was soon back to the youth team and the reserves.

After Billy left, Howard Wilkinson came in as manager and the scramble amongst the group of us – including Gary – to earn first-team call-ups continued. I'd beaten him to a first-team spot but the big disappointment for me was that I wasn't able to follow it up with many more senior appearances. There were a few more but I was at least around the first-team squad for quite a while.

Howard was completely different to Billy as a manager but under him the team moved forward, so much so that we ended up winning the league. I think one of the major reasons for the success was bringing in Gordon Strachan. I know he made a huge impression on Gary. He influenced me as well. He was always someone who, when we were playing in the reserves, would come and talk to you and offer you advice. He would tell you what to work on to improve but at the same time he was quick to praise you. If you needed a rollicking he wouldn't hold back.

Under Howard, Gary broke into the side on a fairly regular basis and then cemented his place for a number of years. Of course, he became an integral part of that fantastic championship-winning midfield of Gordon, Gary McAllister, David Batty and Speedo.

Over the years we stayed in touch, both having also shared the same agent, Hayden Evans. We also enjoyed kicking lumps out of one another when we've been on opposite sides. Once we were out on the pitch our friendship never came into it. We were both highly competitive. We have the bruises to prove it.

We also managed against each other. I was at Blackpool and he was in charge at Sheffield United. So the rivalry extended to the dug-out. I was delighted when he got his big managerial break, being placed in charge of Wales. He was a national hero and so that appeared the logical step. He seemed to take the job in his stride despite not having too much experience. But he was a Wales icon and took his country on from what had been a low point in their history. He laid the foundations for what Chris Coleman achieved in reaching the semi-finals of the 2016 European Championship.

Gary was full of fun on and off the pitch, which makes it so hard to understand what he did. I think I'm like most other people. I couldn't see anything which would make Gary do what he did. He had many close friends and family around him but obviously no-one could see what was going on in his head.

It was such a shock at the time and at least now the mental issues which can strike in football have been highlighted. There is a greater realisation that you have to talk about any problems instead of hiding them. Depression is a horrible illness and has to be treated just as you would a more visible physical injury.

His passing left such a profound impression on people. Two days after his death, we went to Nottingham Forest on a night which proved so surreal. I said to Glynn Snodin just before the game that I couldn't do the team talk because I wanted the players to go out and do it for Gary Speed and his family after everything that had happened. It was just that I knew I couldn't say it because the emotion would have been too much. I asked Glynn to deliver the words, which he did perfectly.

Poignantly, in the 11th minute of the game [the same

number that Gary wore for Leeds], Robert Snodgrass scored with a left-footed shot from 20 yards. I just thought to myself, 'Wow, he's looking down on us.' We won the game 4-0 at the City Ground, a great result. Straight after the game I dedicated the victory to Gary. The Leeds fans were also singing his name. It was an unbelievable night.

I think now, as an experienced manager, I and others in the game do look out more for signs of what some players may be going through, whether there is potential for depression to strike. I think, more and more in football, we are realising that footballers aren't superhuman even if they are sometimes worshipped as such. They are human beings vulnerable to what can sometimes affect so-called normal human beings.

We are now more inclined to look out for any signs that players need help or comforting. It often takes horrible tragedies like the one surrounding Gary to make people realise that football isn't always a bed of roses.

Hopefully, we can learn from these experiences and maybe help save others from a similar fate.

Mickey Thomas

Played for Leeds while Gary was breaking through,
and has struggled with his own demons

I received a phone call early on the Sunday morning from Robbie Savage, asking me if I'd heard the news about Gary Speed. He told me what had apparently happened – I told him not to be so stupid and immediately put down the phone. He phoned me again and repeated what he had told me. I again said he was being stupid and ended the conversation.

I put on Sky Sports and there was nothing on about Gary. I went back to Sav and said he shouldn't go around telling people what he had said to me. Nothing was confirmed. It was all one big rumour.

An hour or so later, there it was on the TV – Gary was dead. I just couldn't believe it. I think I went into shock, I was just completely numb. I'd been with him just a few weeks before at the Welsh Football Awards, where I was presented with an award for services to Welsh football. He came over to congratulate me and we had a good chat. He was just his normal friendly self, someone who was always interested in what you were up to, someone who always had time for you.

When the tragic news about his passing was confirmed I tried to look back to that evening. Had he been any different? Were there any clues to what was about to happen? No, there hadn't been. He was the one person you thought something like this would never happen to. He seemed to have everything, a top job, a wonderful wife, beautiful kids. He appeared the perfect man with the perfect life.

But we all have our own demons and it appeared that Gary kept his well hidden. I've had some bad times and only you know what you're going through. It doesn't matter what you achieve. If you're vulnerable, nothing will save you. Look at Gary – Wales captain, Wales manager, played for some big clubs. None of that though comes easy. It comes with pressure. People don't see that side of it. They just see you out on the football pitch, seemingly without a care in the world. They think your life is perfect. They don't know the other side of what appears to be a glamorous life.

Look at me. When I tell people what I used to go through as a player – being physically sick before games – they can't believe it. On the outside I appeared happy-go-lucky. That really was a shield. At times I would appear cocky with the world at my feet but, believe me, I had some really bad days.

I just couldn't handle playing for a huge club like Manchester United, not after my early days of enjoyment at Wrexham. I couldn't adapt. I was sick before games and, after matches, I saw drink as an escape from the turmoil in my body.

I wasn't a unique case. Look at big stars like Paul Gascoigne, Paul Merson and Tony Adams. All of them took to drink or drugs to handle the pressure. In those days you were generally left to your own devices, whereas now most clubs employ personnel to look after all your needs. There is always help at hand, although sometimes even that isn't enough.

In my era, and to an extent Gary's time, you had to deal with everything yourself. For me, especially at Manchester United, I would start feeling ill and panicky in my hotel room in the lead-up to a game. The night before, I would have to help myself to a few alcohol drinks otherwise I wouldn't get a minute's sleep.

I found it difficult to walk into a dressing room if there were already players in it. I would usually be the first one in the dressing room and the last one out. I just felt intimidated by everything. I would sit in a sauna until everyone else had left. Then I felt able to make my move. Until then I felt completely trapped. The only other Manchester United player who had an idea of what I was going through was Lou Macari, who tried to understand my ordeal. Nobody, obviously, could grasp what Gary was almost certainly going through when we consider what happened to him in the end.

Another problem from my era of playing was we weren't earning the huge money which is going around these days. So when your playing career came to an end, reality would suddenly hit you. What are you going to do now?

You can liken it in many ways to people coming out of the Army. They don't know anything but Army life and so it's hard for many of them to adapt to civilian life. Do we do enough for some of these people?

Sadly, suicides aren't uncommon amongst people who have left the Army and can't integrate back into society. They have obviously been left with mental problems but there doesn't appear to be much real help out there or real understanding.

It's the same in football. Is enough being done to try to address the mental issues which obviously exist in the game? Just because, like Gary, some people appear to have everything, deep down they haven't.

I first got to know him when I was at Leeds United and he was coming through from the junior ranks at Elland Road. Here was this good-looking lad from North Wales starting to illustrate some special talents which would soon take him into the first team. I remember him one day introducing me to Carol and Roger, his mum and dad. With us both coming from North Wales, he felt a bond and couldn't wait for me to meet his parents.

I can remember that day as if it was just yesterday. Shaking their hands and seeing that great smile from Roger, who absolutely loved his football. No-one would have been more proud at seeing his son play for Wales, captain them and later manage them than Roger.

As a player, Gary had many qualities but his heading ability was second to none. He had this incredible leap. That caught your eye straightaway. I just knew he was in for a long and successful career. He wasn't shy but at the same time he was never loud. He just wanted to get on with the job of being as good a footballer as he could possibly be.

He wasn't overawed in the Leeds dressing room despite being surrounded by some high-profile names, players with big personalities.

We had the likes of Vinnie Jones, Gordon Strachan and Gary McAllister. Gary Mac was a great lad. I remember sitting next to him in the dressing room and him saying to Speedo: "Do you know this is the guy [me] whose boots I used to clean at Old Trafford?" Yes it's true, Gary Mac was my boot boy when he spent a short time at Manchester United in the juniors. Until he let it out that day, I hadn't realised.

Once Speedo got in the Leeds first team there was no holding him back. He wasn't a particularly quick player but he was very clever. He understood the game of football from a very early age and was soon respected throughout football.

As a former Wales international, I watched his progress with interest and was never left disappointed. At Leeds there was no better midfield in the country than that of David Batty, Gary McAllister, Gordon Strachan and Speedo.

It annoyed me when there was some criticism of Gary's appointment as Wales boss, some people saying he wasn't experienced enough. I wanted to see him given the opportunity because I knew how much that job meant to him. He soon proved himself more than capable and ended up being the catalyst for the rejuvenation of the international side.

Chris Coleman took it further and all credit to Chris because it was a hard job to take on, considering the awful circumstances. But Gary had undoubtedly laid the foundations.

He was as impressive off the pitch as he was on it. He never forgot his roots, where he had come from. He never failed to come over for a chat if he spotted me somewhere. It's just sad that it all ended far too soon because he had much unfinished business. I would love to know the reasons behind his departure. I doubt whether we will ever find them out.

I feel for all his family, particularly Roger, who is a great guy. He's gone through a traumatic time. He has lost his son, his hero. But both he and Carol kept things going, organising golf days to raise money for charity. Roger once asked me, knowing my background, whether I had ever contemplated committing suicide because he was desperate to understand what drives a person to consider ending his or her life. He is not alone, I feel more people are trying to grasp what depression is all about. It's something which is out in the open, not, as in the past, swept under the carpet.

It wasn't so long ago that I attended the funeral of a former Wrexham player who killed himself, Kieron Durkan. He had been suffering from depression but no-one really knew until it was too late. It makes you realise that we are vulnerable at some time in our lives.

I know Roger has been searching for answers to Gary's obviously disturbed mindset at the time. He, more than anyone, wants to know why. Everyone still would like to know why. His death was massive and still is. He was so highly respected right across the football spectrum. He played the game in the right way.

But depression – if that's what he suffered from – can strike at any point. No-one though really knows in football how to handle it, how to control it. It's unpredictable. It's not like a physical injury which you can see and treat accordingly.

At times, especially at Manchester United, I wanted to go in and see the physio or even the manager and say: "Look, I'm having a really bad time here. I don't really want to be here. I want to go back to who I was at Wrexham. There's too much pressure."

I was still playing a hell of a lot of games but I was shaking like a leaf before many of them, almost too frightened to step onto the pitch in front of the big crowds. I was being sick but I kept all that hidden from my team-mates. I kept all this hidden from my family. Who was going to understand? I was getting paid for something most fans would have happily done for nothing. What was there to be worried about? In my case, plenty.

At least after leaving Manchester United I was brave enough to reveal the main reason – I couldn't handle playing there.

I don't think I would have to go through the same pain or trauma now because clubs do have people on board who can help with most situations. As far as dealing with depression goes, I don't really know. As I say, you can never predict when it's going to strike. When it comes it's just horrible.

There is always pressure. It's whether you can handle it – I couldn't. Maybe in the end that was the case with Gary. He had kept things bottled up and there was nowhere to go. His dream had turned into a nightmare.

He was such a great bloke. After I hit on hard times financially later on in life, if he saw me he would always ask if I was all right for money. One day, I went to his house when he was with Newcastle United and he asked me if I wanted any boots. It was up to me what I did with them, maybe sell them to make a few quid to ease the debts. I ended up coming out of his garage with around 30 pairs. That's how generous he was. When you're fighting for survival, an offer like that can make all the difference. I will never forget his kindness.

He was a very special person – someone who affected many people's lives. Sadly, we didn't realise what was going on inside his head.

Chris Kamara

Played with Gary at Leeds and knew him well through his media work

There are four things I can remember more than anything else in my life.

• I was in Stoke when I heard the news that my mum had died.
• When my dad died I was at his bedside in the hospital.
• When my father-in-law passed away I received the news via a phone call from my wife.
• And when Gary Speed died I was on Sky Sports' Goals On Sunday sofa.

I received a text message from Sam Allardyce saying: "Have you heard the news about Gary Speed, Kammy?" Ironically, the guest on the show with Ben Shephard and I was Vinnie Jones, who of course knew Speedo well from our days at Leeds United together. There we were on that morning of the fateful news – two of his old team-mates on the sofa together.

I didn't believe it at first, I really didn't believe it. Here we were on air, the programme had started and I was trying somehow to take the gravity of a sickening message in. I waited until the advert break and obviously then mentioned it to Ben and Vinnie. I texted Sam back because it still wasn't common knowledge, so you wondered whether it was really true.

Anyway, within 10 minutes the official news of his death broke. It was horrendous. It was still hard to take in or comprehend what had happened. Having known him for 21 years since we first played together in 1990, being told he had committed suicide sent my head into a whirl. I think I must have been in denial, not wanting to believe it – and especially how it had happened.

I was used to receiving text messages during the show because it is watched by a lot of people involved in football.

Managers and players would often send a message through. referring to something they had just seen. This message though made my blood run cold, horrible. Surely it can't be true? Even to this day I still think he is going to come around the corner. I've never met anyone as full of life as Gary. He seemed to enjoy everything to the full. He never seemed to have any problems, he was always so relaxed.

I know he loved his kids. It's the one thing he would always talk about. He did the show a number of times. He was always one of my go-to guys – he would help you out if someone suddenly dropped out at late notice. There was Speedo, Peter Reid, Ray Wilkins, Sam Allardyce, Ray Parlour, Shay Given and David Moyes. They will always come on and do the show if you had to bring someone in at the 11th hour. Speedo would probably be on Goals On Sunday a couple of times a season.

We kept the news to ourselves on the programme because at first it was unconfirmed. What do you do? You can't jump the gun. As much as I trusted what I had seen on my phone we were still uncertain and, in any case, I'm thinking to myself, 'Please God don't let it be true.'

As soon as we came off air the first thing we did was to try and find out more information about Speedo. Vinnie was devastated as well. We both talked about our time together at Leeds when the camaraderie between the players had been something else – very special. Speedo and David Batty were the two jokers in the pack.

To hear confirmation that he had gone was devastating. As I said earlier, it was like hearing one of your own family members had died.

He had only been on the programme around four weeks before his death. I didn't see him but I know now that he was on Football Focus the day before he left us.

I'm now beginning to understand mental illness a lot better because of the facts that are coming out about it. But regarding Speedo, I've yet to really come to terms with it. I don't know how his problems weren't detected.

But on the last show we did together, I would say he appeared happier and more content than I'd seen him. Professionally, he had changed the face of Welsh football. He'd had massive credibility as a player. He was a fabulous footballer – one who had played forever and a day. His first real go at management had been successful. He had a wonderful family. What was there for him to be down about?

The more you read up about mental illness, maybe the more you can understand about Speedo's own mental downfall. But nothing has been proven about the reasons for his death.

Most of the time we don't know what is going through people's heads. It's why I feel very fortunate to be the sort of person I am – someone who really enjoys life. I've played the game, I've coached, I've managed, and I've fallen into television. Maybe if I hadn't have fallen into TV or been a manager then maybe my thought process would have been different.

I'm someone who if one door shuts I've got to try and open another one. But of course even the happiest people in the world have down days. I'm no different. You can have problems with colleagues, problems with your partner, problems with other members of your family. That's happened to me ever since I was a kid.

We as a family had the toughest upbringing in the world. We were the first black family on our estate in Middlesbrough. It was very difficult. Any trouble in the area, break-ins etc, and my dad would be arrested. People would pin anything bad on him. We tended to become hardened to that. My dad always used to say to me: "Don't let them bring you down."

He was in the Navy during the Second World War, having been enlisted from his country, Sierra Leone, and when it was over he was granted permission to stay. When you look at the Windrush situation and seeing some people deported, I think, 'There for the grace of God.'

I got picked on because of my colour – that was the way it was. It was one of the reasons my dad made me join the Royal Navy. He made my brother join the Army. It was aimed at getting us away from any trouble and enable us to both have careers and launch better and decent lives.

The good bit of fortune I had was ending up in Devon, where the Navy football team trained. As a 16-year-old I managed to get into an adults team and played against Portsmouth, scored a couple of goals and the rest is history – I was on the path to a career in football.

I first got to know Speedo after I joined Leeds United. Under Howard Wilkinson, the squad contained tried and trusted players like Imre Varadi, Lee Chapman, Mel Sterland, Jim Beglin, Mervyn Day and Gordon Strachan. The two I didn't know were the two youngsters, Speedo and David Batty. They were two buddies who got themselves into the first team. They were good to be around. They had respect for the senior players. But they had banter and they got away with whatever they could because they were young with plenty of spirit.

Speedo as a footballer was years ahead of his time. I remember for one game Howard made a couple of changes. It was against Oldham on the plastic at Boundary Park. I played centre midfield with Vinnie Jones, Gordon Strachan played wide right and Speedo came in wide left. Even though we lost the game he stood out as our best player on the day. Then on the Bank Holiday Monday we had a game against Sheffield United. It was interesting what side Howard would pick after we had lost at Oldham. He picked the same side and Speedo scored. I can still remember the commentary from John Helm saying: "Go on Gary, get a goal for yourself." And he did. I won the challenge to put Speedo through and luckily that goal is still shown at times.

Sheffield United were our biggest rivals at the time but we beat them. It helped seal our promotion. It gave us belief for the remaining games to end up in the First Division. For a young player to not be fazed with everything that was going on was brilliant. And that was Speedo. It showed his true character.

He had a maturity about him, there's no doubt about that. When you're in amongst all those senior players as he was, it's a sink-or-swim situation. It's hard for a youngster to gel with a team who had seen it and done it. You've got to be comfortable around that or you won't survive. He certainly did more than survive.

Then Gary McAllister was brought in towards the end of the promotion season. I had to have a cartilage operation. I was training throughout the summer to try and get over it. I was the first one to see him. I thought, 'Hell, here I go – another top midfielder at the club.'

The previous season we had played Leicester, who Gary played for. He scored a goal from 25 yards in the first half and Howard Wilkinson had a real pop at me at half-time. I told him Gary wasn't the man I was supposed to be marking. I knew really it was Vinnie's man but Vinnie was keeping quiet. We always later had a review of the game and then Howard realised it wasn't down to me and he apologised. He didn't apologise though for bringing in Gary Mac, which probably cost me a regular starting place.

I would replace David Batty occasionally because Howard thought he needed a break. But he never thought that for Gary

Speed. At times managers have to look after young players. You don't want them worn out after their first season.

Sadly, I left before they won the First Division title. In our first season back in the big time I twisted my ankle playing against Coventry City. I didn't go off because I'd just got back into the team and didn't want to mess up my opportunity. But later, turning onto a ball from Micky Gynn of Coventry, my ankle just stayed in the ground, damaging my ankle ligaments. The injury kept me out for eight months.

The following season – the title-winning one – Howard was pushing me to get fit. We were playing Tranmere Rovers in the League Cup. We won the game. He came to me the next morning to tell me he had agreed a deal with Luton manager David Pleat. I said I wasn't properly fit. He told me to go to listen to Luton because they might make me an offer I couldn't refuse.

I went to speak to Pleaty only for Howard to ring me and tell me that he needed me for the game on Saturday against Notts County. I said okay, so I was substitute against Notts County. Then he said he might need me again the next Saturday when we were due to play Oldham. At least this was giving me time to improve on my fitness. I came on as a substitute against Oldham. On the Monday he said: "Right, you can go." I didn't really want to leave but it was a good financial offer so, for the sake of my family's future, I did join Luton.

So I only ended up playing three games in the title-winning season and one cup game, and that wasn't enough to gain me a medal. I was still pleased that they ended up winning the First Division championship. I had wonderful memories of my time there.

After that injury I was never the same player, to be honest. Eight months out with an Achilles and ankle ligaments took its toll.

I went to the end-of-season celebrations for Leeds becoming champions of England. I had been invited, which was a nice gesture. I was in there with the lads enjoying it.

My friendship with Speedo continued beyond Leeds. He was to become a regular on our Goals On Sunday show. I would meet the guests on the Saturday night and have a couple of drinks. With Speedo, I would always ring him to find out what time he was arriving so we could enjoy a few beers together.

I was in constant touch with him over the years. I haven't really looked closely but I know his text messages will still be in my phone.

To this day, it's still hard to get my head around what has happened to him. I've spoken to Alan Shearer, who was really close to Gary, two or three times about Speedo and I'm still shaking my head. Nobody I know seems to have grasped why it happened.

I went to the funeral with Howard Wilkinson and Gordon Strachan. Gary McAllister was supposed to join us but we couldn't find him anywhere. He had taken a turn for the worse over Gary. The whole thing still baffles me to this day.

4

OUR LIFE AS A FAMILY

*'As a person he was very vocal. Everyone
had to hear his opinion. I would say my bit
but in the end Gary's opinion had to stand.
That was just the way it was'*

I wasn't working now. I was a proud mother, having given birth to Ed, and ready to buy a home in Rossett. We moved in there in the June and moved out the next February because Gary became a Newcastle player.

With having Ed, I hadn't been to that many Everton games but I know Gary had become somewhat disillusioned with a few things at Everton which led to the move to Newcastle. I think I was so absorbed with motherhood with Ed being our first child that much of what happened with Gary as a player at Everton passed me by. I just know there came a point where he felt it was time to leave.

When Gary got to the end of his time at any club it became very obvious. He would become irritable, obvious that he had itchy feet and wanted to move on. He loved Everton as a football club but things weren't right for him and I could tell he didn't want to remain there much longer. At any club you can sometimes outgrow it or feel you don't fit in. Gary was never someone just to stay for the sake of it. For him there was always a natural tipping point. It came at Everton, even though it was the club he had supported as a boy.

I couldn't believe it though when he told me his next club was going to be Newcastle because I know in the past I'd told him that if there was one club I didn't want him to move to it was Newcastle. It seemed that players there spent all their time partying. One day he came in and told me: "You're not going to believe it but start packing, we're off to Newcastle!" I thought, 'Oh no, here we go.'

Kenny Dalglish, who Gary had tremendous respect for, signed Gary but sadly Kenny wasn't there for too long.

I'm now pregnant with Tommy so we've got a young Ed and Tommy on the way. Gary found us a place to rent which to me was completely in the wilderness, near Rothbury in Northumberland. It was lovely but really more of a holiday home. We spent almost a year there before buying a house in the Morpeth area.

He absolutely loved his football at Newcastle and we made loads of friends. Tommy was also born in the North East to complete our family. We felt very settled there, which is so important when you have young children.

I eventually started changing my mind about the precon-ception I had with Newcastle, although at first there were some hectic nights out. I seem to recall that his first day up there after signing was a day out at Newcastle Races with the boys. I was still in Chester thinking, 'Here we go!'

They were a good bunch of guys. We got to a stage where we would go out as couples after most home games. Gary was really friendly with Alan Shearer, Rob Lee, Steve Harper, Shay Given and Warren Barton. Sometimes John Morris, an ex-cricketer, and his wife Sally would join us.

We'd go into Newcastle or visit a great Italian in the village of Ponteland called Rendezvous. It was all quite special because we all got on so well. If it was someone's birthday they would treat the whole gang for a meal – another excuse to go out.

It was disappointing for Gary when Kenny Dalglish left. As a footballer you are always nervous about who the next manager would be. Ruud Gullit came in and Gary got on quite well with him and liked his training methods.

At Newcastle, Gary reached two FA Cup finals – although they ended up losing against Arsenal and Manchester United. I went down to Wembley for the Manchester United game. I can remember David Beckham being with Victoria, his future wife, in the players' lounge after the match.

Gary enjoyed his days in the North East. He was someone who was always fully committed to his job. Football becomes the main focus. You can't avoid it because everything has to revolve around the football and the club you are playing for. At least having a family gives everyone something else to focus on – to not make things so intense. It allows you to place things into perspective.

I still laugh now when I recall Gary's face one day at the dinner table. Both of the boys were urging him to play football with them once the meal had been finished. He told them he would if they just gave him five minutes to finish off his evening meal. One of them said: "I'll be you, Dad, and you be Alan [Shearer]." You should have seen the look he gave them. I don't know if he actually went out to play with them after that comment!

As a person he was very vocal. Everyone had to hear his opinion. I would say my bit but in the end Gary's opinion had to stand. That was just the way it was. Most times I respected his opinion because it was fair and he would look at most things objectively. I like someone with a strong character who has opinions. You knew where he was coming from.

His great hobby was golf. On a day off at Newcastle a game of golf was usually on the cards. He also loved quizzes. He would never miss A Question Of Sport. He loved taking part in it. He loved the feeling of winning – at anything. You would often hear at home, "Daddy's won!"

Gary couldn't wait for holidays to come around, he absolutely loved us all being together exploring different places. We also had a holiday home in Saint-Tropez, in the south of France. It was on a golf course and was very nice. We'd usually go there one year and the next year we'd go off somewhere new.

We had a great time with the boys discovering interesting places in Canada one summer. Gary loved his holidays from a young age. It was always his big escape. He would always plan it so well.

I've been looking at some photos to remind me of some of the places we have been to. There's photos of us all in Barbados, the Bahamas. We stayed in a hotel called The One And Only

Ocean Club where one of the James Bond films was shot. I think the boys' school pals were a little envious of their holiday destinations. They loved every moment of our time together in the sunshine discovering new places.

Gary was almost like a tour guide. He loved organising and had a brain that absorbed any knowledge, and so he was in his element during our holidays. He was an intelligent man and also wanted his children to learn. Summer holidays for him weren't about sitting on a beach. So quite often I'd come back from our holidays without a sun tan!

It was about cramming as much new information into his head for Gary. I think it was the same when he went on football trips for his clubs and Wales. He'd be the one urging others to join him and discover some of the history of the area. He found everything so fascinating. He preferred somewhere he didn't know so that he could broaden his mind. He also knew it would be good for the boys' education in the long run.

Bobby Robson followed Ruud Gullit and, strangely, it seemed that Bobby didn't know too much about Gary being sold to Bolton. Gary was ready to go. I think he felt it was the right time to move on again. There was no way Gary could spend anytime on the substitutes' bench – that would completely frustrate him. That wasn't Gary. He wanted to be out on that pitch playing all the time.

Gary arrived at Bolton, where Sam Allardyce was the manager, in time for pre-season training and after at first almost being distraught at him telling me he was signing for Newcastle, I was now reluctant to leave the area which had produced so many happy times. I felt so settled there and had made some really good friends.

The boys were now six and seven, and settled at school. It was the summer holidays and I wanted to enjoy them in the North East. With that in mind we decided that Gary should commute for a while. It was hard on him because he had to book into the hotel which was actually situated inside Bolton's stadium.

It hit him hard. He was missing his family and so during the October half-term we joined up again. He had found somewhere to rent in the Frodsham area, just outside Chester. It was a lovely modern apartment. We got the boys settled into a school in Chester.

We wanted life to be more settled, with the lads now dependent on their schooling. This is the other side of being a footballer's wife. It's not all about material things, it's about trying to do your best for a family which is growing up. I don't think many people realise how much time you spend alone because playing for a successful side takes them away for a considerable amount of time.

Especially if you are living away from where you were brought up, having no parents around or no old friends to call on can at times make it a lonely existence. What you see on these footballers' wives shows on the TV is very different to how it can be. Often, I didn't have my parents just around the corner and you miss that and the family things you generally take for granted. You can often feel segregated.

Now we were back with both of our families on hand and eventually moved into a house in Rossett, an area we had lived before. Although packing up the house in the North East was quite sad because it prompted some lovely memories.

At Newcastle I had become very friendly with a girl called Gill, who lived in the same village as ourselves. We started running together and the children were also of a similar age, so we bonded quickly. The kids were close and treated one another as cousins.

I said to Gill one day: "Let's do the Great North Run." I thought while I was living in the North East it would be nice to have a go at running in it. It was something to train for. She said she would train with me but wouldn't be entering the race. In the end she did do the run with me. We ended up doing it two years running. The first time I finished in two hours and four minutes. The second time I did it in less than the two hours – and it came after one of our typical Newcastle nights out with friends.

It was just lovely running down all the country lanes close to our homes. It was a case of put the trainers on and go. Another friend who was inspiring when it came to fitness was Sian. The three of us had wine, fitness and children in common.

I enjoyed the experience of the Great North Run so much that I suggested to Gill our next mission was to run in the London Marathon. Her instant reply was: "Absolutely not!" Again she agreed to help me train for it. Again we both took part. I know Gary was very proud of me doing that. It gave me a focus. I didn't have to work and anything I did try to do would be insignificant monetary-wise but I still needed some focus. It kept me sane because I had these two little boys to look after. I came back feeling tired but at the same time refreshed. We always did Monday, Wednesday and Friday. But running was like a drug and if we could sneak another run in at the weekend we would. That would mean paying someone to look after the children but it was well worth it.

Sadly, Gary couldn't watch me in the London Marathon because he had a game. But having done it myself I persuaded him to run in it. I told him it had been one of the best feelings ever and that he should do it – and he did. I know that halfway around the course he was interviewed by Sue Barker. He told her he had been inspired to take part because of his wife. I think you can still find that interview on YouTube. I think once he had done it he realised what an achievement it had been for me to finish.

When I crossed the finishing line I just wanted to cry. As a teenager I had watched it on the TV. I thought to myself that one day I would like to be there taking part. I noticed there were lots of older runners. If they could do it, why not me? It was just fantastic realising my dream. My time was four hours, 29 minutes and 33 seconds. I will never forget that and I know I enjoyed every step of the way. I can't remember his exact time but I do know he said it would have been quicker if he hadn't have stopped to go to the toilet! Once you stop it's hard to get going again. I think he did it in around three hours and 50 minutes.

I was only just half-an-hour over that, which made me feel even better. I just wanted to cry tears of joy once I had crossed the line. A feeling of pure elation. It was also nice to doing it with Gill. She had been dogged by an injury and so we decided that we would run the first 18 miles together and then whoever felt that surge of energy could go on alone from there.

At 18 miles I couldn't wait to step it up and luckily I never hit the wall. It was a wonderful achievement – something I had waited to do for years.

Next up was the New York Marathon. I had decided I wanted to do one more marathon before I reached 40. Gary was at Sheffield United at the time and Simon McCabe, the son of club owner Kevin McCabe, was doing it. He asked whether I wanted to take part. It was short notice but I told Gill we were going to do it. We both went out there. We stayed at the Ritz-Carlton and I almost lost a friendship because Gill found it so hard, especially with 21 miles of it up a hill. I did it in around five hours but it was a lot harder than the London Marathon.

Having both ticked that box, it's now the end of our marathon running. The two boys, who are living out in the USA now, realise it was quite an achievement having become familiar with the race.

I might whizz the dogs out for a little run now and again but, to be honest, I feel I've done everything I wanted to do as far as running is concerned. I might do something like a three-miler but nothing longer now.

Gary didn't say too much to me about the marathons but evidently he would tell everyone at work what I was doing, which was nice.

When Gary was at Bolton I didn't see many of the games because the two boys were now playing football and Gary felt it was imperative that they were supported. His football wasn't important. His football was a job while, for the boys, it would hopefully give them enjoyment and discipline. It was the same when he joined Sheffield United – it was almost impossible to fit him and the boys in if they were playing. And in Gary's eyes they came first. They were also coming to an age where if they weren't playing they would rather spend time with their friends instead of watching their dad.

Whenever he had some spare time – which wasn't very often – he would try and pop down to do some coaching at Hawarden Rangers, a junior side in the area where we had both been brought up, because the boys played for them. The other lads in the side loved Gary spending some time with them, passing on advice and encouragement.

He wasn't a pushy parent. Both Ed and Tommy enjoyed a natural love of football. Ed got a cap for Wales Schools later on and Tommy represented the Independent Schools Football Association at Under-16 and Under-18 level.

We decided not to move house when Gary joined Sheffield United, although at one stage it looked like we might after Gary was made manager. He asked if we could move to the Sheffield area and I think my face fell on the floor. I'd had enough of packing up and starting all over again somewhere. But while we contemplating whether to move again, Gary was named as the Wales manager.

It was just as well for me because I think I would have had to agree to another move because he was finding the trips to and from Sheffield hard, and was having to spend a couple of nights in a hotel.

It had been a natural progression for him moving into management with Sheffield United. He had done some coaching because his back had gone, which meant surgery. He came back from a game at Cardiff in absolute agony. He

Making a mark: The Deeside Primary Schools' FA team in 1981. Gary is pictured in the centre behind the Welsh Shield alongside his team-mates, with friends and family behind

One of the boys: Gary *(pictured in the white jumper)* 'gatecrashing' Louise's 13th birthday party

Early days: A young Gary and Louise

Young love: Gary and Louise during an early holiday together and *(above)* a picture of Gary starting out at Leeds

Happy together: Gary and Louise full of smiles on their wedding day

Rising star: *(Right)* An early cap for Wales. *(Above)* Scoring for Leeds against Everton at Goodison Park in 1991

White hot: *(Left)* Celebrating an equaliser for Leeds against Tottenham in 1991 with David Batty. *(Below)* The 1991–92 First Division champions

The class of '92: Lining up with his Leeds team-mates – including Gordon Strachan in a kilt – to show off their title winners' medals

Heroes: At the front of an open-top bus on a tour of Leeds

Seeing the world: Relaxing outside the team hotel before a game against Armenia and *(above)* lining up for his country in 1995

Winner: Lifting the First Division trophy for Leeds

Royle appointment: With Everton manager Joe Royle in June 1996, delighted to be signing for the team he supported as a boy

Dad time: *(Below)* On holiday with sons Ed and Tommy and *(left)* with the boys in the USA

Head master: A spectacular header against Tottenham in 1997, the only goal of the game

Leading the way: Celebrating a goal against Barnsley *(above left)* and battling with West Ham's John Hartson in 1997

My ball: Putting the brakes on Arsenal's Emmanuel Petit

Marathon man: Signing in at Newcastle and *(above)* with Sir Bobby Robson on his 400th Premier League appearance

All smiles: Enjoying the moment with his team-mates after scoring his first goal for Newcastle against Barnsley

Heat of battle: Toe to toe with Wayne Rooney in Wales' World Cup qualifier against England in 2004

needed an operation and never really recovered to be able to play to the standards he had set. It's why he did more and more coaching and then was offered the manager's job.

He was an absolute nightmare when he was recovering from the operation. He was now at home during his rehabilitation and we had Sky Sports on all day, every day in the kitchen. One day I'd had enough and asked whether we could turn it over to another channel. He had a right bellow at me – it was 'no' in a very impolite way. To say he wasn't a very good patient is an understatement but at the same time I don't think I'm a very good nurse. He was completely frustrated. He was never any good at doing nothing and was miserable with it.

To be fair, he was coming up to 40 and had played longer than virtually everyone else. But that didn't seem to make any difference. It was a case of trying to keep out of his way.

But thankfully along came the Wales job, which was a dream for all of us. It meant that we could spend more time as a family because he didn't have the same commitments as a club manager. You're not away all the time – there is a better balance to your life. There's not much balance in football generally. For the first time in his football career he had some spare time on his hands, which was great for the boys and I. Before, he had been so absorbed by his football commitments, which at times dictates and runs your life.

It's a routine as a player where you are told day in, day out, when to sleep, when to get up, when to eat, what to eat, where to go, what to do. Then as manager of Sheffield United there had been so much pressure trying to make an impression in his first managerial job where you are having to think weeks, months ahead. So when Wales came along it was so different. At last we could all look forward to more family time.

Every weekend he would go to watch one or more of the Wales players in action and would also take Ed with him. Tommy was never bothered but Ed would go. He would always dress up, look the part, to be with his dad. He absolutely idolised him. I think this is what helped Ed to meet and greet people. He is still the same now. When he meets someone he always shakes their hand and says it's nice to meet them.

Tommy was more into his boxing and became a junior English champion. He would also prefer to be with his mates then go and watch games with his dad. But Gary really encouraged him with the boxing. He thought it was a great sport. I hated it. I could never really understand it. But it kept his fitness up, especially in the summer when he wasn't playing football.

I did watch him box and that was the only real time I have seen Gary so nervous. Watching his son box, he couldn't relax at all. Seeing him so nervous made me try and relax more, otherwise Tommy would have seen two nervous wrecks. I soon realised how much skill there was in boxing. It just wasn't one great blow-out in a ring. It's a very disciplined sport. The relief was he won most of his bouts. He never came out worse for wear – there was no disfiguring of the Speed good looks.

Gary was proud of him. Tommy has given it up but has talked about taking it up again sometime again for the fitness side of it.

With the Wales job, once Gary knew he was in charge of his country he was straightaway making notes about how he was going to change things. What he wanted implemented. He was itching to start and make an impact. I would listen to him. I just admired his enthusiasm. Anything he did, he would throw himself into it 100 per cent. There were no half measures with Gary – and that was in anything he did. He was so determined and passionate about managing Wales. He was champing at the bit.

Gary was never someone who wanted any of his achievements to be mounted on the wall or anything like that. It could be international caps or shirts. I would get them framed but he wasn't bothered. The only thing he ever asked to be displayed was the team sheet of the time Wales played England with Gary as manager. He was so proud that he wanted that up on the wall because beneath the Wales line up was Manager: Gary Speed. So it went on the wall.

As far as I was concerned, being manager of Wales took away a lot of the pressure of family life with someone who was often away or working all hours. There could now be some balance. It seemed perfect, the ideal scenario.

The year before he died he was awarded the MBE. I remember him saying to me that he didn't think he was worthy of the honour, he hadn't deserved it. When the news came through the post he wondered whether he should accept it.

Even when we all travelled down to Buckingham Palace for the award, he felt there were so many there more worthy than him. There were people who had fought in wars and there he was a footballer.

Then...

5

BENEATH THE SURFACE

Bobby Gould

_Gave Gary the proudest moment of his playing
career after making him the captain of Wales_

I was at the Swansea v Aston Villa game working for Sky
Sports. I walked into the media room and somebody told
me: "Speedo has gone." "What do you mean he's gone?"
I replied. Then he blurted out that he'd committed suicide.

Nothing in this world can forearm you for news as stunning
as that. I stood still and I simply couldn't take any more
information in. I was in the middle of the room stuck there
like a frozen doll – I couldn't comprehend anything that was
going on around me.

It was like a nightmare you desperately wanted to end. I

couldn't control my thoughts or even my movements. I was lost, not knowing really what to do or what to say. I decided to continue working but really you are not there. You are not really functioning. How could you be after receiving the shock news of Gary's sudden and unexpected death?

All that was going on in my mind were the flashbacks to when he was my captain in the Wales team I managed for four years in the Nineties. It was me who gave him the captain's armband – something I know he was very proud of.

Once the game had finished – not that I can remember too much about it – I got into my car ready to drive to my Bristol home when Sky Sports rang and said they would like to do a piece with me talking about Speedo, and asked if I could I divert to the national stadium in Cardiff. The camera crew were waiting for me and I did what had been requested. What was really surreal is that my wife Marjorie would have woken up in New Zealand to me talking about Gary Speed's passing. She always turned on Sky News to keep up to date with what was happening back home. She was visiting our son Jonathan, a coach at Wellington Phoenix at the time, and his family.

How unreal would that have been? Marjorie waking up and seeing me recalling some of my times with Speedo, who sadly was no longer with us. It would have been a hell of a shock to her as well because when I was manager of Wales she would often travel with us and so got to know the players and staff.

She's 12,000 miles away and there's her husband on the television breaking the terrible news about Speedo. At least being in the car, travelling from Swansea to Cardiff, I'd had some time to gather my thoughts. During the journey I kept on thinking, how sad – and why?

It was an easy decision to make him the Wales captain. He was a natural leader and would always speak his mind. He was a great person, someone who had stature.

Making him my skipper didn't save me from a few blasts. He wasn't afraid to stand up to me if he thought I'd made a mistake or he wasn't happy with the tactics. He just wanted Wales to be successful and didn't tolerate second best.

I do think he sympathised with my task, to an extent. I'd taken over at a time when many of the senior players like Ian Rush, Mark Hughes, Neville Southall were coming to the end of their international careers. I was the one charged by the Football Association of Wales to chart a new path with younger players.

He was never afraid to challenge me. But I felt more comfortable with Gary as captain because ultimately we both wanted the same thing – to make Wales more professional. If that meant at times him jibbing at me, it was worth it in the long run.

Looking back, and being completely honest, until I took the Wales job I'd had no experience of international football. You quickly realise it's completely different to anything else you've done in the game. Too often you would take charge of players who were completely shattered from their weekend endeavours with their club sides. Maybe, at times, my enthusiasm was too much for them. I wanted to give everything and make Wales successful. They just wanted some rest.

I think Speedo could see what I was aiming at maybe more than some of the others. Although I don't think he saw that when he gave me a right mouthful after we had lost 4-0 to Tunisia. We were in the midst of a rebuild but to hell with that, he demanded more from some of the players and then turned on me, accusing me of being in charge of a pub team.

He calmed down and later thought maybe he shouldn't have said that. But it didn't bother me. You always knew Speedo would have his say in front of you, never behind your back. It was always nose to nose, fire would be coming down both sets of nostrils. I accepted that. The trouble is, as an international manager you can't bring in new players through the transfer market. You are stuck with what is available and, to be fair, it was a time of transition. It's not the easiest thing in the world to replace an Ian Rush or a Neville Southall.

You have to wait for young players to come through. We also needed more Welsh players to gain experience in the Premier League. Too often we were calling them up from the Football League or from Premier League reserve sides.

A good example of that was the progress Gareth Bale made in later years once he was a regular pick for Spurs in the Premier League after moving from Southampton.

I think one of my biggest let-downs was becoming Wales manager without any international experience as a player. It took me time to adapt and fully understand the business of being in charge of international players. It needs a different approach to club management. You definitely get more stick as an international manager. When things went wrong with Wales I was quickly reminded of my English heritage and I would be doing everyone a favour by returning there!

As a player, Speedo was wonderfully talented. He never let up throughout his career. Those exacting standards were always met, even when he reached his thirties. The challenge as Wales manager was, could I make him an even better player on the international stage? As captain he always led from the front, even in training. One thing I quickly took on board were his complaints that often the team would stay in sub-standard hotels and the travelling arrangements weren't always the best.

To ensure things improved on that score, I took it upon myself to be the advance party looking to vet potential hotels abroad. I would look for the best training areas and how we were going to travel. So I don't think in the end Speedo could have had any complaints because I tried to make sure everything was top drawer. I took great pride in changing the perception that Wales did everything on the cheap.

It was no surprise to me that Speedo went on himself to manage Wales. Look at the experience he had gleaned as an international player – something, as I admit, I didn't possess. Then take a look at some of the managers he had played under – Bobby Robson, Kenny Dalglish, Howard Kendall. You couldn't help but gain valuable knowledge, especially with the intelligence he brought to the game.

But I know he had his fights with the Welsh FA during his short time in charge of his country. There would be no stopping him. He would always fight for the best. As a player he helped educate me during my time as Wales manager with his ideas and commitment.

I like to think, even though we had our moments, we respected and appreciated each other. I'd always told him I was available for a chat at any time. Even though I resigned after four years through frustration with certain issues, I still wanted Wales to do well. I wanted him to be successful just as I had wanted Mark Hughes to make a real go of it as Wales boss. It's often about timing and whether you have the right players at your disposal. I think Chris Coleman went in at the right time. Who wouldn't want Gareth Bale in your side, for instance? I think Speedo had made things more comfortable for his successor.

Some people probably see me as a failure as Wales manager but the one legacy I'm really proud of is the coaching courses the Welsh FA now run. Thierry Henry and Mikel Arteta have recently acknowledged their importance in helping them achieve their top coaching badges.

I helped get all that off the ground during my time as Wales manager. I'd got all my coaching certificates through the English FA and wanted the Welsh FA to expand their coaching courses. They were so successful that they have attracted the likes of Henry, Arteta, Patrick Vieira and David Ginola. So I think I might have got something right. The list of those who have successfully completed the courses there is quite phenomenal. I know it's something Gary was very proud of as well because it helped put his beloved Wales on the map.

Joe Royle

FA Cup-winning Everton manager signed
Gary, a boyhood Blue, in 1996

I was driving to Oldham on family business when one of my sons rang me asking if I'd heard that Gary Speed had died and it was suspected suicide. Without one ounce of exaggeration, I nearly veered off the motorway. Then the news started coming out about the tragedy, although it was still very hard to comprehend – a beautiful young man, a certainty sometime in the future to manage a Premier League club, probably Everton. Who knows why it happened? Gary had raised the profile of Welsh international football. Everything seemed to be going in the right direction, career-wise. It was a shock to us all.

I remember really noticing Gary for the first time at Leeds United in that great midfield of Gordon Strachan, Gary McAllister and Gary Speed. When they won the league he was magnificent. He could leap in the air and was a good header of the ball. There were few better left-sided players at the time.

After I became Everton manager I couldn't wait to buy him. Barry Horne was moving into his thirties and we needed to freshen it up. It turned into one of the easiest deals I've ever done. His agent, Hayden Evans, came on to me and said: "Joe, I've got to tell you I've got instructions here to just get the deal done." Leeds didn't want him to leave but obviously Gary thought he needed to move on. When he knew of our interest he was delighted. The terms were agreed in no time at all after we had settled a fee with Leeds. So in he came.

He was great to have around in the dressing room. He wasn't as vocal as someone like Neville Southall – I don't know anyone who was! He didn't have the dry wit of Dave Watson but you knew he was there. He also had a great smile which would lift you. It was an infectious smile. I will always remember that constant smile on his face.

He was terrific for us and it all looked set fair. But a few months later I left after a disagreement with the chairman Peter Johnson. I had wanted to sign the goalkeeper Mark Schwarzer because Neville Southall's time as an Everton great was coming to an end. Peter thought we had spent enough. I also wanted to sign Tore Andre Flo from a Norwegian club. I had speaking to his agent, Rune Hauge. He had advised me to take Flo's mate as well, a decent defender, to help him settle so I agreed a £2 million fee for the pair of them. Peter didn't want to do it because he said Flo would be available on a Bosman free in the summer. He actually ended up going to Chelsea for nothing but we had missed out.

We had words but Peter didn't want to sack me. However, for the first time we had lost faith in one another. We hadn't had a blazing row. We came up with this stupid decision that we would part company.

At the time his number two, Cliff Finch, was at a party in Barbados. Dave Whelan, the Wigan chairman, went up to him and observed that Everton would now be looking for a new manager. "No we won't, we've got a great young manager," replied Cliff. Dave insisted that I'd gone. Cliff hadn't known a thing about it. I left, Howard Kendall came in and I was left totally surprised when Gary eventually joined Newcastle. I couldn't understand Everton allowing somebody as talented as Gary to leave. I've heard since that Gary had very valid reasons for wanting to go.

I think on the football management side he was a shoo-in to become Everton manager at some point. When you have managed a country, it usually follows that you're in line for a top Premier League job. You've seen it with Mark Hughes,

Chris Coleman, Roy Hodgson and Sven-Goran Eriksson. Having international manager on your CV, you can't fail.

Gary had been a top player, which included being at Everton. He had gained the right experience. Managing Wales isn't the easiest job in the world. You've got a limited number of players to work with, some of them plying their trade in the lower divisions. You have to give great credit to what Chris Coleman achieved after succeeding Gary as Wales manager, which wouldn't have been easy.

After his death I got to know his parents Roger and Carol very well. Through them you know he would have enjoyed a great childhood. Roger has called in at times at our house with Gary's two sons, Tommy and Ed. As a proud grandfather he would take them around everywhere – nothing has been too much for both Roger and Carol.

The whole thing is a mystery. A total mystery. I can't believe how he could have left two boys who he adored behind in the manner he did.

I hadn't known Roger or Carol before his death but I felt that I had to, in time, speak to them. Having once signed Gary and been his manager, I felt it right to get to try and get to know them. I rang Roger. It was both hard and easy. Hard in the fact that I was meeting two grieving parents but easy in that they are two lovely, caring people. Both devastated of course. Roger was initially probably handling things better than Carol.

It's ridiculous, isn't it? Usually when you meet someone who has just been bereaved, without thinking you just blurt out: "How are you?" I think that was my opening phrase. The answer should be "ruddy terrible" but people are polite, as were Roger and Carol. I've spoken to Roger on a number of occasions since and I know he still has no idea why Gary decided to cut short his life.

Roger is a little sad now that his grandsons are away in the USA because they were his and Carol's anchor to help them through the tough times at first. Everyone seems to have been heartbroken. Gary's death has touched so many people. It's really incredible.

But this behemoth we know as football has a habit of shocking you, just when you think you've been in the game long enough to have seen and experienced everything.

Gary's death certainly falls into that category as far as I'm concerned. Here we had for all the world a handsome man with a beautiful wife, a great football future in management ahead of him, a lovely house, great children, terrific parents – his star was rising and then all of a sudden...

Barry Horne

Former Wales captain and a teacher at the school Gary's two sons attended

I was at home on the Sunday morning. I don't have any papers delivered and never put the TV on as soon as I get up. I'd received some weird text messages, people saying they were really sorry. The first couple of texts never explained what they were sorry about. Then the phone calls started about what had actually happened. I put the TV on and it's all over the news. It's a feeling of utter disbelief. Initially I thought he had been involved in an accident. The suggestion that it was because of something else didn't hit home until later in the day.

In the end it was so someone I knew from Sky Sports who filled me in to what had actually occurred. To find out that he had killed himself was an even bigger shock.

I'd been with him the day before. He had been watching one of his sons, Tommy, play football at King's School, Chester, where I am a teacher. I think after that he was heading off to appear on Football Focus. We had a chat and he was clearly making plans for the future in his job as Wales manager. He was talking about possible staff changes.

I can clearly remember what he was wearing. As usual he was laughing because he had a tremendous sense of humour. There was not a single clue of what was to happen. In fact, quite the opposite, he was excited about implementing some of the future plans he had been discussing with me.

His other son Ed was also a pupil at the King's School. Obviously as a teacher you have a duty of care and responsibility with any child you teach. But I'd known Gary's two lads for a number of years, Tommy more so because Ed left for another school, Abbey Gate. It was natural because of my friendship with the family that I would try and look out for Tommy. Roger, Gary's dad, had said how important it was to keep a special eye on him. That wasn't difficult because he was such a great lad.

Even when Gary was alive, Tommy being his son, you try not to be biased but at times you can't help to be pulled towards them. He was the best footballer. He was a great kid. It's human nature that you maybe favour one ahead of another. I don't care what anyone says, you can't treat everybody exactly the same all of the time – it's impossible. To his credit, Tommy went on to achieve more or less what he was striving for. He left us to go to Repton School on a football scholarship because he was outstanding. He displayed great fortitude and character and remarkable resilience after what had happened to his dad. Achieving what he did was an amazing testimony to his character. He's now a big, strong, fit lad.

It was obvious that Gary doted on his two lads. He was brilliant because although he adored them, at the same time he put them right. He wasn't blinkered. He brought them up strictly. They had impeccable manners. For want of a better phrase, he didn't blow smoke up their arses. He kept them well and truly grounded. They were his kids but he saw them for what they were. He was very careful not to spoil them. Some parents think their son is always the man of the match, the best player. Gary was definitely not one of those.

I first really got to know Gary after he was called up by Wales for his first international away trip. We were flying off to play a game in Copenhagen against Denmark and we all met up at a hotel just outside Chester. He'd made his senior Wales debut as a substitute against Costa Rica in Cardiff. Because I was the captain and he was a young player new to the international scene, it was normal that he was told to room with me.

He'd already made his mark with Leeds, so of course I knew something about him. My first impression about him on actually meeting him ran true right throughout his life. He was well spoken, very polite, very respectful, very humble, obviously good-looking. His sense of humour didn't really come out then because he was still a young lad and he was in a strange environment with some very big football names in the

Wales squad. His sense of humour and confidence emerged later. I would never say he was nervous because there was a quiet confidence inside him, even then. That definitely wasn't cockiness, just a quiet inner belief. He had been brought up well, had been well educated and was doing very well at Leeds.

It was the same growing confidence you might see in a young Ryan Giggs or young Mark Hughes. Already, he was a well-rounded personality. It's ridiculous to look at any young player and predict what they are going to be like in future years. As footballers you don't do that. We leave that to the media! You look at what he's got and think to yourself, 'Yes, he's got a chance.' You accept them for what they are at the time and get on the training pitch and see what they can do. Everything then grows organically.

Ryan Giggs came more into the 'certain future star' category than Gary at that time. He had a chance of being one of the greatest players while Gary was a good player who was doing really well, progressing and had all the attributes to be a decent player. He ended up being more than that but, most importantly, remained true to his upbringing.

John Hartson

*Former Wales team-mate of Gary's who fought a
battle with cancer following his retirement*

I was covering Swansea City v Aston Villa for BBC Five Live on the Sunday. I walked through to the press area in the ground and I bumped into Bobby Gould, who both Gary and I had played under when Bobby was the Wales manager. Gary was in fact his captain. Just before I was about to enter the media room, Bobby came up to me and put his arm around me and said: "John, Gary has taken his own life." I went: "What? Who? Gary who?"

He said Gary Speed had killed himself. I couldn't believe it. I couldn't take it in. He placed my head on his shoulder and I don't think I could have moved for almost two minutes. I simply couldn't bring my head out of his grasp. I felt completely numb.

I knew I wouldn't be able to work. I couldn't concentrate – nothing else mattered. To be honest, I couldn't believe the game went ahead because the news was breaking about Gary's tragic passing. After all, he was the Wales manager and the game was being played at Swansea. The atmosphere around the ground was understandably subdued.

Then you had Shay Given, one of Gary's closest friends and Aston Villa's goalkeeper, bawling his eyes out, although by then I was in my house. I had gone home. I couldn't work. Bobby had told me to be professional and carry on doing my job. I told him there was no chance of me working. My head was in bits. I drove the few miles to my home in a complete daze. How I got home safely I'll never know.

My mother came around to the house because I had phoned her to tell her the news, although by then it was all over the various news channels. She gave me a little glass of whisky just to calm me down a bit. We ended up spending the whole afternoon just reminiscing about Gary, hardly believing we were talking about him no longer being with us.

I watched bits of the game on the TV, although it was all a blur. I wasn't bothered about it or who had won despite being a Swansea supporter. The phone never stopped ringing, no-one really able to believe what had happened.

On the Monday I appeared on a programme on S4C, which is for Welsh speakers. I was asked to meet up with Malcolm Allen, who had played alongside Gary and was a big friend too. We did the programme and it was a very poignant, emotional show. It was quite tearful and it was difficult to get through it without completely breaking down.

A few days later I made contact with Gary's dad Roger. He was devastated. So, of course, was his wife Louise and Gary's mum Carol. With Roger we both talked about the effect Gary's death would have on his sons, Tommy and Ed. I didn't really see Louise until the tribute game a few weeks later in Cardiff and I gave her a hug. It was all so surreal and still is. It's such a sad loss.

I played with Gary for the best part of 10 years for Wales. For a time he was my captain and was someone I looked up to. He was a great lad, a man's man. He was first at the bar, first to go for a night out – he loved the evenings out.

He had film-star looks but was a real bloke. He loved a game of golf. He looked after himself, had a wonderful career. We all admired him. As a player he would always have a bottle of water in his hand, always aware of what was good for you, what was good for the diet. He was just an inspirational leader, an inspirational captain, an incredibly inspirational man.

He commanded respect from everyone without asking for it. For instance, under Mark Hughes he went to play at left-back despite being one of the best midfield players in the Premier League. Sparky wanted Gary to play there so he could get the likes of Robbie Savage, Mark Pembridge and Simon Davies in the side. The front three would usually in those days be myself, Ryan Giggs and Craig Bellamy.

That meant me never going too deep because when those two broke with speed I'd have to be with them over the halfway line – otherwise I would be left behind! We had so much fun together, travelling around the world. He just loved playing for Wales.

He was a few years older than me so his close friends in the team were Andy Melville and Chris Coleman, a massive mate. He first roomed with Dean Saunders, then Chris. But he always had time for the younger players like myself and Craig Bellamy, Danny Gabbidon, Robbie Savage and Giggsy.

Since his death I've spent a lot of time with Roger at his house in Hawarden. We've spoken about the good times with Gary. If I was ever in the area I would phone him to see if he was in the house and I would go and enjoy a chat.

At first, at every opportunity Roger was invited down to Cardiff for Wales games. Chris made him feel very welcome and we knew Gary would have liked that. I was one of Chris's assistants when he took over. All credit to Chris because it was in many ways the impossible job being expected to take over as Wales manager in those bizarre circumstances.

It wasn't easy at first because the results went against him and you worried about his future. In the end he decided to do things his way and forget the past. It was no use keeping harping back to Gary's reign. He was gone and it was up to Chris to forge his own path.

That crucial decision helped him become arguably the most successful Wales manager ever, leading his country to the semi-finals of the European Championship. Not that Gary was ever forgotten. We'd often sit up late into the evening with a bottle of wine and the talk would turn to Gary. We'd share some lovely stories. It would always end up getting a bit emotional. Terry Yorath was a great manager and Mark Hughes was fantastic but, in terms of achievements, no-one did better than Chris.

It's strange to think that I fought like hell to beat my cancer and feel lucky to still be here whereas Gary, who appeared to have everything, ended his own life. It's hard to contemplate but all I can think is that he was in a very dark place at the time.

It was 2009, two years before Gary's departure, when I faced my own life or death situation. I had discovered little lumps on my testicles four or five years earlier but in true bloke style had ignored them. Because I had left things, all this led to a tumour. It was virtually too late because the cancer had spread to my lungs and brain. It's a little galling when the surgeon stands over you asking you to sign a bit of paper which means that if I didn't wake up again he couldn't be held responsible.

Luckily, I did survive the six-hour operation on my brain and when I came around my mum and dad were at my bedside looking at me with a huge bandage around my head. My dad asked the surgeon Dr. John Martin if the operation had been a success? I'll always remember the reply. "Don't worry Mr Hartson, it was just a bit of plumbing." My dad gave him a big hug. I'd just retired from playing and was starting in the media but my negligence made it a huge battle. I've got two whopping big scars where they went into my ribs to get to my lungs. The scars are there for everyone to see.

And in March 2018 much of the nation witnessed the ravages of my cancer battle when I agreed to bare all for a live television remake of the film The Full Monty, when a group of unemployed men decided to become strippers.

I don't think I've ever been so nervous. I was even forced to undergo my first – and last – spray tan. But it was all for a great cause, with the proceeds from an appeal which ran alongside the show going to a number of cancer charities.

Because of my dice with death I have a different outlook on life, a different perception. I'm a lot calmer now. I appreciate time with my family and kids because it came so close to being taken away from me.

I'm in a good place. Gary obviously wasn't. To this day I have no idea why he did what he did. But whatever it was – if only he had just put his hand out and spoken to someone then maybe he would still be here today.

There have been lots of rumours, which is inevitable in any unexplained sudden death. Some people have questioned whether he was gay. Well I certainly don't think that was the case. Even if he had have been – and I know he wasn't – it wouldn't have mattered. Everyone loved him.

Did he take something to his grave? We will never know. Things have been said over the last few years but I would like to remember him as a real top-class bloke.

It's a crying shame for his boys and Louise. But I don't hold any grudges over his drastic actions. It's just a huge shame he is not around any longer. It's so sad he couldn't find a way to express any dark feelings he may have had. They always say when people take their own lives that the person is in a very dark place and nothing else matters.

He couldn't have been thinking straight because, for a start, he idolised his two boys. He worshipped them. He had a gorgeous wife, Louise, but no-one knows what was going through his head at the time.

I have shared many cups of tea with Roger and Carol, his parents, and they have no idea why. I don't think anyone has any idea.

He had been on Football Focus the day before his death and he didn't look any different to me. Some people since have said he looked a bit agitated. I couldn't see that. What I hate is all the rumours. There's only one person who knows the real truth and that's Gary. Maybe it's good that we'll never know because I want to remember him how he was.

If there was a problem, I'm just disappointed he didn't ask for help because there was so much love for him, so many great friends who adored him. If he had picked up the phone to someone, then whoever it was would have been there for him like a shot.

I shouldn't be here. I've been blessed that I've been able to watch my children grow up. As well as winning the fight for life, I've left a gambling addiction I once had behind. I've been clean in that respect now for more than seven years. In the past at times I have been very down, maybe depressed. I think most people suffer black moods at times.

I've had some great heights, last-minute winning goals for Celtic against Rangers, a big career move to Arsenal, big games for Wales. I've never got too carried away, I've tried to be balanced.

In Gary we looked upon him as being strong, very stable, not up and down like the rest of us. But maybe he was suffering inside. But he never shared that. That really eats me up.

Ian Rush

Liverpool legend grew up in the same area as Gary and played alongside him for Wales

I had only been speaking to Speedo the day before he died. I was in Dubai in a car with a mate called Ray who had been rung up by Speedo. I think Speedo was on his way to appear on Football Focus. Ray handed the phone on to me. Speedo said he was planning to come out to Dubai with his family around Christmas time and he was asking me what it was like. He was going to do a bit of coaching but would use the time as a family holiday as well. I told him it was a great time of the year to come out and that his family would love it.

The next morning I received a call from John Richardson, a journalistic mate, who asked me whether I'd heard the rumour going around that Speedo had hung himself. I told him to not be so stupid as I'd only been talking to him the day before. I just thought it can't be true, it's just one horrible joke. Very soon the awful news was confirmed.

I just couldn't believe it. I knew him well during our time

together at Wales and, as I say, I'd only just had a normal conversation on the phone with him. He seemed happy enough with everything. It was hard to take in. You start asking yourself, was there anything that suggested he might ever do what he eventually did? I've got to say as far as I was concerned there was absolutely nothing. His career was certainly going in the right direction. He always looked as fit as hell. There were no signs of any deep-lying problems at all.

Even before I met him for the first time, I knew all about him because we are from the same area in North Wales. I also knew he used to deliver Kevin Ratcliffe's newspapers – nearly always late! You quickly get to know if there are any decent young footballers in the area and his name was always cropping up.

Then I watched him break into the Leeds United side and he looked a fine young player. He then progressed into the Wales side and that's when I began to get to know him. Straightaway you could see he had a great left foot and the thing I really liked about him was he always managed to get some great headers in at the far post. He was exceptional in the air. He seemed a really good lad.

I used to room with Kevin Ratcliffe and Rats would take the mickey out of him for once being his paper boy. He didn't mind and would join in the banter because he had a great attitude, a really good sense of humour. He always seemed a very happy person and it was fantastic to have him around the Wales squad.

He always produced the goals which helped take some of the pressure off the likes of myself and Mark Hughes. He always worked hard and gave 100 per cent, and quickly adapted to international football. It was obvious he loved playing for his country. Once he became a senior player, I know he became more vocal in the dressing room. When I was there he was only a young player and never really said a lot.

I noticed his confidence had grown when I went to Newcastle. He was already there and was one of the established players in the side under Kenny Dalglish. He was definitely more vocal. As a young Wales player, I think he had looked up to senior players like myself. At Newcastle he was more experienced and would have his say. I was in and out of the side.

He seemed really happy. He was made up that one of his big mates from his Leeds days, David Batty, was there. He was big friends with Alan Shearer. Bats was amazing. He didn't like football – he would never watch it. But he was a great lad and the two of them were really close.

Later on it was nice to see Gary appointed as Wales manager. I was the elite performance director for Wales and, through that, saw what he wanted to achieve. With Osian Roberts, a mutual friend and top coach, he wanted to have a continuity of play all through the age groups, the Under-21s and through to the senior side.

I'd mentioned to Gary about the work Osian had been doing – something I'd witnessed for two years – and I know that he was quickly impressed when he saw for himself what the Under-15s and Under-16s were achieving. Speedo though discovered that, under Brian Flynn, the Under-18s and Under-21s were doing things differently.

Brian wanted to carry on with his system but Gary was strong and wanted to impose his methods because, after all, he was the Wales manager, which came with big responsibilities and big expectation.

He told Brian if he wasn't prepared to change then he would have to look for another job. It ended up with the Football Association of Wales not renewing Brian's contract because they went along with Speedo's belief that you needed continuity through the ranks to have any chance of being successful.

It was a brave decision to have to make because Brian had done well, results-wise, with the Under-21s and had helped bring a number of players through to the senior side.

Speedo laid the foundations for Chris Coleman to build on after his passing. The good thing was that no-one forgot that. The fans, for instance, sang his name during the great run to the semi-finals of the 2016 European Championship. They still sing it now.

You have to give Chris a lot of credit because it would have been really hard for him when he took over. He didn't have the greatest of starts and, in fairness, he ended up having to make his own decisions, just as Speedo had done.

The infrastructure implemented under Gary was still there but Chris needed to construct the buildings. At Liverpool, for instance, Bill Shankly had laid the foundations but it was Bob Paisley who took the club to a different level.

When you look at the sad end of Speedo's life it takes me back to when I left Chester for Liverpool as an 18-year-old in what was a world-record transfer fee for a teenager.

The first year at Anfield, I hated it. You are in a strange environment, you're young, people are always taking the mickey and all that. A move like that either makes or breaks you. It was on the verge of breaking me. I wanted to go back to Chester.

I'd only seen the players I was getting changed next to on TV. Some of them were my boyhood heroes. I was suddenly in the same dressing room, stars like Alan Hansen and Ray Clemence.

You're just a kid and they are taking the piss out of you. I knew I was at the club because I was good enough, otherwise they wouldn't have bought me. But it all comes down to mental toughness. That's what it is all about in football, the mental strength needed to survive.

When I became older I would take the mickey out of young players. You are testing them to see have they got what it takes when the pressure is on. It was about trying to engineer a good team spirit, something which was traditionally at the heart of Liverpool's success.

It's not just about your ability as a footballer. It's also about your mental capabilities. I know when I was unhappy in my early days at Liverpool I bottled it up. I didn't tell anyone, I just kept it all to myself. I just took it on the chin and tried to get on with things. More should be done to help players who go through bad times.

We also have to remember that probably only about one or two per cent of promising 16-year-olds are going to make it as professional footballers. What about the remaining 98 per cent? There will be some who will look upon themselves as failures and be vulnerable to bouts of depression. We've got to show them that there is another life out there away from football.

At the same time young players have got to realise that

you sometimes have to go one step back to go two steps forward. People also develop at different ages. In my opinion, it's getting the balance right. Yes, you have to be caring, but not to go over the top and molly-coddle kids.

Nowadays, kids of 13 or 14 have their football boots cleaned and polished for them, whereas when many of us were looking to make our way in the game we were cleaning the boots of the professionals and being made to do other chores. It seems that this discipline has gone out of the window.

You need a happy medium where players with any real problems are helped but there are also disciplines in place to help you grow and mature as a person.

You have to treat people differently. Some people can take a bit of a hammering where others need an arm around them to help cajole them. At Liverpool, Bob Paisley would never shout at me because he knew I was quiet. But someone like Terry McDermott would get an earful because he knew it wouldn't harm him. It's about knowing the individual.

Gary came up from a similar background to me where you had to fight to get what you wanted. That's why it makes it even harder to understand how it ended for him. On the outside everything seemed fine but it appears now that he kept some things hidden. It's another glaring example of not knowing what some people are going through.

The trouble is, as so-called macho men who play football, it's hard to tell people your problems – you would get laughed at.

Hopefully that attitude is slowly changing as football is now more aware through instances like Gary's that it's dangerous to bottle things up.

Here's me saying you should tell your parents or close friends of anything that is bothering you – but I didn't when I was having that miserable time in my first 12 months at Liverpool. I just got on with it and, luckily for me, things worked out. That though isn't always the case.

Robbie Savage

*Taken under Gary's wing after breaking into the
Wales squad, the pair became close friends*

Just three weeks before he left us, Gary and Louise had been on the front row watching me on BBC's Strictly Come Dancing show. I'd just done the jive and I came over and we shared a high-five. It was great to see the look in his face that showed he was so proud of me.

It was a great atmosphere and I know that he loved Strictly. During that week I was in contact with him quite regularly because I had a few personal issues and Gary was someone I could always go to for advice. He was always so accommodating because we got on so well.

You could ring him on any football issue, on anything at all. If you had a problem he was always there for you.

I was in bed on the Sunday morning in the hotel we used for Strictly. I had got through to the next round of the show the previous night, which had been very pleasing.

Then came the telephone call from Quags [Tony Quaglia, the Wales kitman]. He delivered the tragic news that Speedo had left us. I told him it couldn't be true. He'd been on

Football Focus the previous day. I'd been with him three weeks earlier and he had been in great spirits. "It can't be right," I replied.

By now Quags was crying his eyes out, telling me the horrible news was true. I still couldn't believe it and then the news broke during the day. It was just mind-blowing. It was incredible to think that just three weeks ago he had been enjoying himself on the front row at Strictly. The next week I'd been speaking to him as mates, having a laugh.

It just wasn't sinking in. Here he was with his management career with Wales going great, he had been there with Louise on the front row of Strictly seemingly without a care in the world. Then there was his Football Focus appearance. Nothing made sense.

I then went ahead and did BBC Radio 5 Live's phone in programme Six-O-Six which was scheduled for the Sunday night. It ended up being a tribute programme to Gary. It was so tough to do with my emotions still red-raw at the time. To be honest I was all over the place. I didn't want to pull out of the show. I wanted to do it in memory of Gary.

As everyone could imagine, it was so emotional. There were some heartfelt messages from the whole spectrum of football. It showed how much he was loved and held in such high esteem by everyone, no matter who you supported.

It was powerful, powerful radio and I'm just pleased I went ahead and did it even though my head was in a mess and I was completely heartbroken. I knew that people from all over football would want to pay their respects. I hadn't been wrong. It was so moving at times and emphasised just how many respected and loved Gary.

It also brought it home just what a waste it was losing Gary at such an early age. It's something that resonates to this day. It wasn't a case of trying to delve into the reasons why it happened – it was a nation mourning a fantastic person.

On the outside he looked so amazing, someone who appeared to have everything. A beautiful family, a managerial career going well, a fun guy to be around. So on the outside looking in, you're thinking how can this have happened?

Even seven years later it sends your head into a whirl as you ask yourself, why Gary, why? Like everyone else who was close to him, you wish maybe we could have spoken to him and possibly helped him with any problems he had. It's just a sad scenario, especially with his close-knit family.

We can only guess the reasons for Gary doing what he did. Did he have mental health issues? – we just don't know. I think we all go through tough times but many of us aren't very good at opening up and looking for help. That can come through just offloading to someone. It can't always be your family.

I probably come across as a larger-than-life character with no worries. But like most people I can have my down moments. There's been a lot of speculation surrounding Gary. The only certainty is that he must have been in a very, very low place to have ended his life. The state of mind you must be in – it's just incredible really.

It was hard for me when I finished playing. There's too much time for reflection and you can feel terrible. It's something many people can't understand. They look at players who have finished their careers and think, 'Oh he'll be all right he's got pots of money – what can go wrong?' I'm afraid that isn't always the case. It can be tough having to adapt after only knowing one thing for most of your life – playing football.

My admiration and affection for Gary started when, as a young player at Crewe, I was called into the Wales squad. Here were all these big stars like Ian Rush, Mark Hughes and Neville Southall.

It was Speedo who took me under his wing, helping me, encouraging me. I was in awe of most of them but he was the captain and he went out of his way to help me. It was way beyond his responsibilities as Wales captain but that was Gary.

One of the last talks with him was suggesting that if I was ever in the area where he lived, why don't we go for a game of snooker somewhere? He told me to just come around to his house! And if I ever fancied a swim – come around to the house! But with Gary it wasn't said in a bragging nature – it was to put me at ease and have a laugh.

He was a great character as well as being a great captain. He would also, I'm sure, have gone on to become a great manager. His departure has been a great loss to the game in addition to the horrible consequences for his family and friends. He was a privilege to be around. He looked after me and I'll never forget that.

As long as I've known him he always had leadership qualities. But he was different to some other leaders because he always had your best interests at heart. He questioned things on behalf of you, which paved the way to be successful at management.

Look at what he did with the Wales squad he inherited. It

was incredible how he built it and thankfully Chris Coleman was able to continue that work. To his credit, Chris moved it on to achieve the success they enjoyed at the 2016 European Championship.

Gary had his thoughts on how he felt the game should be played. He had the immediate respect of the dressing room. He would have gone on to great things as a manager, there's no doubt about that. He wasn't afraid to have his say – but if you were a young player he would never hammer you. He would speak to you in a way which wouldn't crush your confidence.

I remember an ex-Wales captain – and he will remain nameless – in one of my first appearances for the country he tore me apart. Gary would never do that. As a captain later on for some of my club sides I took some of Gary's qualities on board.

During your career you meet some captains you respect and others you don't. It's about harnessing the good points and making sure you don't repeat the bad ones.

I think a good captain realises there are different personalities in the dressing room. You can't treat everyone the same. Some players you have to put your arms around. Others you have to have a real go at them to extract what you want. You've also got to realise it's about trying to look after the whole squad, not just the 11 who are playing that day.

It's also as a captain how you communicate with your manager. Gary was brilliant at that, as was Ryan Giggs when he captained Wales. I've learned from a lot of captains I've played under but, without a doubt, Gary was one of the best. He had that human touch.

It wouldn't have mattered if he was the captain of Manchester United or Crewe, he wouldn't have handled the players any differently. I always knew if I could emulate those attributes I would have at least half as good a career as he enjoyed.

I had an inkling that after enjoying the day he came to watch Strictly Come Dancing, he would have loved a go at it. I'm sure he would have done well as he did well at pretty much every challenge he set himself.

Like everyone else I imagine, at times I look back and wonder was there anything he did or said that could have foretold of the tragedy which would unfold. The answer is there was nothing. Not a single thing gave me a clue, especially when you recall he was on Football Focus the day before.

At Strictly we had enjoyed a drink together with Louise. He was laughing and joking as normal, giving me the traditional stick over my performance. It was just great banter, certainly not coming from someone who was going to abruptly end his life.

It's just such a terrible loss. He was an ambassador, a role model. There was so much ahead of him. Look, for instance, at the group of Wales players he left behind and how they have progressed. I remember when we played against England at Wembley and gave them a real scare. You thought then, 'Wow we've got something going here under Gary.'

I thought Chris Coleman handled a very difficult situation well. He never forgot to praise Gary, which was fantastic. He took it on and eventually placed his own stamp on the team and can be very proud of what he achieved.

It was a lovely touch inviting Gary's dad Roger to the Euro finals. It was very moving and a great example of the Welsh sticking together. Gary triggered the momentum and Chris built on Speedo's legacy.

We can't speculate about why Gary took the action he did. But what I do know is the most important thing if you are ever feeling low is to talk to someone. If you've got issues, pick up the phone to someone. There are so many helpful organisations out there and, of course, you've got your mates. But it's having the courage to admit you need help, someone to lend an ear while you try to unload.

I've done that. It's not embarrassing. You've got to be able to speak and if you are prepared to get things off your chest then there is help out there. I've discovered that and I've always told other people to do the same.

Don't forget, sometimes you can't confide your worries or fears to a family member. But there's always one person out there you know who would be able to listen. As I say, sometimes it takes guts to tell someone your problems. But the worst thing is to keep those dark thoughts to yourself. They can build up and build up to a point where people can't see a way out. If you can speak then it makes it easier.

Neville Southall

Former Wales and Everton goalkeeper who has been
supporting research into suicide bereavement

I was on my way to Cardiff and I missed around four telephone calls on the mobile from the Wales kit man, Tony Quaglia. I then received a text message from one of my mates which said, 'R.I.P Gary Speed.' I thought to myself that this was some sort of sick joke. Who's doing all this? A minute later, Quags finally got through to me and asked if I had heard the news about Speedo. Obviously I hadn't. I was, by a coincidence, driving to a hotel where some of the Football Association of Wales people would be.

I bumped into them and by then the news had been confirmed. Most were in a state of shock, just like everyone else who had known Speedo.

I then started to think back and tried to recall his facial features. Had he been happy? Had he been sad? Did he have sad eyes? Was he depressed? You go through all that but of course you are looking back, and whenever you do that and reflect on the past you can always look at it in two different ways. That was my problem. I couldn't work out why had he had done what he did. He could be a bit quiet. He was a perfectionist. He had a great work ethic and work attitude. But could he let things get on top of him? Nobody knows what goes on behind closed doors. But after assessing everything, I have to say I never noticed any clues to the eventual sad outcome.

As a player, if we lost a game for Everton or Wales, he could be quite moody. But then again, a lot of us were like that so really that wasn't anything out of the ordinary. He was always striving, time after time, to get better and better. He liked things to be done properly. He would get the hump if that wasn't the case. But does that make him a candidate for taking his own life?

Recently, I've been involved in helping the push to produce

the first-ever survey in Britain on the reasons behind people taking their own lives. It is being conducted by Sharon McDonnell, from Manchester University, who was moved to undertake this task after losing her brother through suicide.

It's understood that suicide is now the biggest killer of young men. And the numbers are going up and up. She also organised a conference to discuss these alarming statistics and try to find a solution to a serious development.

Back to Gary. I do know through studying this subject that perfectionists get fed-up easily. But on the other hand he had a good dry sense of humour.

As a player, I don't think I've seen anyone capable of playing well in so many different positions. That also illustrated he had an incredible football brain and appeared on the surface a very strong individual. But the more I go into all this stuff the less things make sense. There is no set formula when it comes to taking your own life. It can come out of nothing, a spur-of-the-moment decision. What I've also found out, being involved in helping with the survey, is that just before someone decides to end their life they are at their happiest for some time. You know that once you have ended the torment you will be at peace. It's the end of their journey.

Gary and I came from an era where you would never want to show you had been hurt, physically or mentally. If you confessed to any supposed weakness then you were called a girl – or worse. Thankfully, things are changing. In our era it was basically, 'You're a man so get on with things.' That's how it was done. Gary was a deep-thinker and now you wonder, was he hiding anything?

I still remember when he first joined Everton, following a game he announced he was going for a cool-down and asked who was going to join him. I thought why not, I might as well go. Nobody else really did cool-downs in those days. Usually at Everton there would be him, myself and Willie Donachie. He brought that to the club. It had previously been a case of have a cup of tea and bugger off home. He believed in it and that was transferred to Willie and me. He was ahead of his time in many ways as a player. I believe Howard Wilkinson at Leeds had left a huge impression on him.

With his professional attitude he could have been anything he wanted to be. Look at what he created when he managed Wales for that short time. He sparked them to greater things under his successor Chris Coleman. One of his innovative moves was to bring in the Dutch coach Raymond Verheijen. What Wales had lacked for some time was the arrogance which says you are a good team.

For some years before Gary came in, Wales players never felt they were any good. With Raymond at his side they started to instil the confidence needed – a new belief. It was a work-in-progress but now the players were starting to believe they were on the road to becoming a really good team. The legacy of that was for all to see in the 2016 European Championship when Wales reached the semi-finals. It was great because they had gone on to believe that they belonged on the world stage.

Gary's was a terrible loss both personally and professionally. I'm convinced he would have gone onto be a really great manager. He had been a great captain and would have replicated those skills in management.

As a young player for Wales I always felt he could have been a magnificent sweeper. I know at times he would move to left-back but I saw him next to the two centre-halves who would do the marking and he would be able sweep up and bring the ball effortlessly out of defence because he could really play. He could have ended up as one of the best sweepers in the world, a Welsh Franz Beckenbauer. He would have been absolutely magnificent there.

He could do everything on the pitch. He was a good organiser. People respected him. He was a winner, good man-manager and had a great football brain. He had all the physical attributes. At times I think these skills were wasted when he was playing for Wales.

But back to what he finally did, choosing to end his life. There have to be reasons. It's why this huge survey on the reasons for suicides was conducted this year. Is there anything to flag up that we can all look out for? I used my Twitter account to try to help Sharon find some answers. I helped her get in touch with people like Frank Bruno and Norman Whiteside to try to push the survey.

When people talk about suicide and say that although they've had low moments – let's face it we all have depressive thoughts at times – but wouldn't contemplate anything as drastic as taking their own life, they are thinking as a totally rational person. But if your mind is spinning out of control then there's no thought about what you are leaving behind or that it might be a selfish act. The only thing they can see is to end it all.

What Gary's death points to me is that he did have some mental health issues. Just because you are a good-looking fella, seemingly with the world at your feet, doesn't safeguard you from bouts of depression. It's often said by other people about those who seem to be well off etc: "What's he got to be depressed about?" You can't choose to be depressed. Depression chooses you. You don't decide to wake up one day with depression. It just happens.

Maybe with Gary there was something always lurking in his mind – something which had spooked him in the past. Maybe as someone who had such high standards and everyone expected him to keep to them, it would at times have been very tough mentally to uphold them.

Look at Paul Gascoigne, for instance. A great footballer who has battled with depression over the years. He had no direction in his life once he finished playing. There was pressure when he was playing, and he wasn't too bad attempting to handle that, but as soon as he finished nobody gave him a pathway to enjoy himself. He should have gone straight in as a youth coach at a club. He would have been brilliant working with kids.

Gary was a completely different character. He was a great captain and role model but sometimes that can become wearing as well. Could he switch off as much as he wanted to? Even being with his two lads who he idolised, you can only switch off to a certain extent. If there is something troubling you it will always be there in the back of your mind. Things can grind you down after a time.

He always looked great on the outside to everyone but, let's face it, you can't be like that on the inside every hour of the day. When you're a perfectionist it's hard to settle for anything less. He was good-looking, everyone respected him so much so he was like a film star doing the job, but at times everyone puts a mask on as they go out of the door.

And Gary sometimes had those sad eyes which indicated that there had been trauma at some stage in his life. But that's now looking on in hindsight. I didn't really feel that at the time when I was with him. It's only now looking back and dissecting certain things.

One thing I would like to see is the Football Association and the Professional Footballers' Association taking a good look closely at mental issues in football. Every club should, for instance, have a mental health officer.

I also believe that the coaching badges now should be split. Half should be as it is now, being able to teach people in whatever sport. The other half should be teaching how to look after people. Look now in sport at the different sexualities, mental health, worries about bullying. There's so much other stuff going on that you need a holistic badge. This is how we are capable of looking after each individual. What to look out for. It hopefully means that people like Gary don't slip through the net.

It's pointless if we don't look closely at the other side of sport – the mental pressures etc. Whether it will ever happen, I don't know. But I would think now you could have grounds to sue if a player's mental wellbeing isn't looked after by a professional football club. A young player's life can be ruined by just a few wrong misplaced words like 'queer', 'bender' or a racial term. Now is the time to say that you can't coach unless you also know how to look after people.

If a player comes to you with a problem away from things on the football pitch, how can you deal with it if you haven't been taught yourself?

6

The autobiography

TYNE TO MOVE

*'The few weeks between leaving Everton and
returning to Merseyside as a Newcastle United
player had done nothing to dampen down hostilities.
The abuse reserved for me was unbelievable. I've
never known anything like it during my life'*

With things having gone sour for me at Everton, Newcastle United's interest in me was flattering, especially with Kenny Dalglish being the manager. Although I am Everton through and through, Kenny had always been a hero of mine. As a Liverpool player he was incredible. My dad also idolised him. He didn't really support any team but he enjoyed watching Liverpool and Kenny couldn't do any wrong as far as he was concerned.

Despite the accusations which first came my way from the Everton supporters who until now wouldn't have known some of the reasons for leaving the club I had followed as a boy, I didn't join Newcastle for a penny more than I had been earning at Goodison Park. I went to the North East because I felt it was a step up in my career. Newcastle were higher up in the Premier League. They were the same reasons why I had joined Everton in the first place from my first club Leeds United. I hadn't gone to Everton because I had supported them from the terraces, I had joined them for professional reasons.

It didn't take much for Kenny to sell the club to me. I had wanted out at Everton and Newcastle was an ideal next move.

I couldn't wait to get started although it was a little surprising when, after playing in a central midfield role for Everton, Kenny asked me to play wide left, a position I hadn't really occupied since my First Division championship-winning days with Leeds United. I struggled to make a real impact at first and it took some time to win the Newcastle fans over.

I don't think it was helped by the fact Newcastle were in a bit of a lull and many of the fans were still harking back to the golden days under Kenny's managerial predecessor, Kevin Keegan. Newcastle had just struggled to get past non-League Stevenage in the FA Cup. The team were struggling for form.

What was even worse on a personal front was that just a few weeks later Newcastle faced my old club Everton at Goodison Park in a league game. It was only my third match for the Toon and, of course, the dust hadn't had anytime to settle and I knew emotions were running high. I hadn't wasted any time moving my family up to Tyneside. But that hadn't stopped the hate mail reaching me at St. James' Park. Having been captain of Everton, I was seen as some sort of Judas figure for seemingly walking out on my own people. Many of the letters were oozing with vitriol. They were warning me that they knew where I lived and to watch my back when I came back to Goodison. Well I didn't have to wait long to find out whether these menacing messages were just bluff or the real thing.

As a precaution, Everton erected some steel shutters to protect the players' entrance. The club knew it could turn nasty when I arrived with my Newcastle United team-mates. Those shutters are still there to this day. 'The Gary Speed gates' the locals call them! I must admit the approach to the ground inside the Newcastle coach wasn't my most comfortable journey – far from it. I was nervous, really apprehensive. This was a completely different, nerve-racking experience to the ones that had gone before at this famous ground. Before, there had always been a tinge of excitement, whether it be as a young kid anticipating watching my heroes or as an Everton player looking forward to trying to gain three points.

Now here I was sitting on the edge of my seat, the enemy. The few weeks between leaving Everton and returning to Merseyside as a Newcastle United player had done nothing to dampen down hostilities. The abuse reserved for me was unbelievable. I've never known anything like it during my life. The Everton fans banging on the coach and shouting obscenities as it arrived at the entrance to the ground were obviously well fired up. It was really horrible and hard to understand how I had created so much hatred. "Shithouse Speed" was one of the calmest chants aimed at me. As I say, until they've read this book none of them would have appreciated one of the main reasons for leaving the club was the physical state of the manager.

It obviously didn't get any better when I walked out on the pitch. "There's one greedy bastard" boomed around the ground. The volatile atmosphere did get to me. I just couldn't get it out of my mind. Of course, I had been expecting plenty of animosity but I honestly couldn't believe the ferocity and plain nastiness of it. It definitely affected me and I was nowhere near my best. We didn't play well as a team either but managed to grab a goalless draw. There was more stick as I got back onto the coach. Everyone wanted to have a go at me and yet my friends, many of whom were and still are Everton fans, had understood my reasons for leaving. Not that it was any consolation but Duncan Ferguson, who had been an Everton icon following his move from Rangers, suffered the same treatment when he returned to Goodison as a Newcastle player after his transfer to St. James' Park.

At least over the years things have calmed down. People realise I am still an Everton fan at heart and now I am treated well whenever I go back to Goodison to watch a game or as a TV pundit. I certainly know which sort of reception I prefer!

It took some time for the Newcastle fans to accept me because although we reached the FA Cup final against Arsenal in May, we hadn't really been setting the Premier League on fire, eventually finishing 13th.

They really got on my back during a game against Crystal Palace at St. James' Park. I passed back to Steve Howey, one of Newcastle's central defenders, he slipped, Palace scored and we were 1-0 down. The next time I touched the ball there was a chorus of loud booing. It wasn't nice to hear but in many ways it was the best thing that could have happened to me because after that incident I always strained every sinew to try and get the ball back if I lost it or if I made a mistake. That is something Newcastle fans demand.

For some strange reason the fans didn't really take to Kenny despite everything he had achieved in the game. Probably much of that was to do with him taking over from Kevin Keegan, who had been like a Messiah to the Toon Army. It was a hell of an act to try and follow. It will be the same at Manchester United when Sir Alex Ferguson finally calls time on his reign. Who would fancy following in his huge footsteps?

Kevin had been a hero with the Newcastle fans because of the buccaneering style of football that he encouraged. They won games 4-3 and the supporters had lapped it up. When Kenny came in he decided to tighten things up in defence and I don't think that went down too well. Kenny also had this guarded persona in front of the cameras and so people might have thought he was dour compared to Kevin, who has always worn his heart on his sleeve. Kenny though, away from the public eye, is a fantastic bloke. He is down to earth, very approachable and with a great sense of humour. We always had a laugh and a joke with him during his time at Newcastle. It's just a pity that things didn't really work out for him there.

Although he was calm and relaxed most of the time, he wasn't soft. He certainly wasn't afraid to have a go at players if he felt the stick was needed. It was my first game and I was a bit taken aback when he had a real go at Robert Lee, one of the senior players. But if he said something, you responded and would go out and do it.

Kenny would always join in the training sessions but for such a great player, with the reputation he had, he was really hopeless. He might have been one of Scotland's finest but honestly he couldn't do a tap in training. I suppose he was getting on a bit though!

It was a good dressing room, full of characters. Alan Shearer was one of the main men. In fact, most of it was made up of the old guard, players from the Keegan era like Philippe Albert, Steve Watson, Rob Lee and David Batty, who I had known from my Leeds United days. Ian Rush and John Barnes were also there, brought in by Kenny.

There was a relaxed style with Kenny but there was always respect for his methods. Alongside him was Terry McDermott and Alan Irvine. Terry was absolutely brilliant. I think he is underestimated by the football world. Some people perceive him as a joker, a sort of dressing room court jester. He's a lot more than that. His role was understanding the players. He was always upbeat and lively and knows the game inside out. The players loved him. If anyone had a problem they would go to Terry. Every manager needs a Terry McDermott to be successful.

Despite not being revered in the same way as Kevin, Kenny still took us to an FA Cup final. It came just four months after I had joined the club. We were facing Arsenal and it was amazing to see Wembley Way a sea of black and white. The FA Cup has always been special for Newcastle supporters and 1998 against the Gunners was no different. They were wandering around Wembley at the crack of dawn singing their songs, unbelievable. Sadly for Newcastle, that was just about as good as it got. We were poor, the game was poor and Arsenal were the better side. Nicolas Anelka and Marc Overmars grabbed the goals. We didn't really turn up as a team.

It was still a huge shock, however, when in August of the next season Kenny was gone, sacked just three months after taking the club to Wembley. I was driving to training unaware of the breaking news. I even went past two TV vans which were obviously going in the same direction, towards the training ground. I was wondering, what was all that about? We all quickly found out – Kenny had lost his job. I was really upset because he was a good guy and he had been one of the reasons I had moved to Tyneside.

Ruud Gullit came in to replace Kenny and the atmosphere changed within the club pretty quickly. I don't think Ruud and I hit it off straightaway. He left me out of the side a few times shortly after he took over. It was the first time I had been dropped. Nothing like that had ever happened to me at Leeds or Everton. Ruud was very good tactically. He knew how to deliver what he wanted from players and I learned a lot from his methods. At least when I was playing I was back in central midfield.

I fell out big style with him on one occasion when he wasn't honest with me. Before one game he pulled me to one side and asked whether I could do him a favour by playing at left-back because Stuart Pearce, who usually played there, would be unavailable because his wife was having a baby. I agreed that I would providing it wouldn't hamper my chances of continuing in the central midfield role. I was at left-back in the final training session. Reporting for the game on the Saturday, the last person I expected to see was Stuart Pearce. I asked him, was he playing? "Of course I ruddy am," was his blunt reply. Ruud never pinned the team up until 1.45pm so I had a bit of a wait. Sure enough, Pearce was at left-back but

Speed was nowhere to be seen in the starting 11. I told Gullit the decision was "a f*****g disgrace". I wouldn't have minded so much if he had pulled me to one side and explained that Pearce was, after all, available and I was missing out. Although I blasted off at him, I didn't throw the toys out of the pram. I just worked harder in training, listened to what he had to say and in the end I didn't miss too many games.

We played Coventry City away and I was surprised to see Nolberto Solano, normally a right-sided player, being named as one of our central midfielders. I was on the substitutes' bench again. We went 1-0 down and Nobby was hauled off after just 20 minutes. I felt really sorry for Nobby but it was my chance and I was going to try and take it after being asked to replace him. I scored and we went on to win 5-1, and that was the turning point for me under Ruud. He also bought Stephen Glass, who was a left winger, from Hibernian so that meant I would stand or fall on what I did in central midfield, which suited me.

Ruud fell out with a number of players during his time at Newcastle because when he left them out he never really explained the reasons why he was doing it. I enjoyed a good midfield partnership with Rob Lee until he fell out with Gullit. Rob was banished to train with the kids, which was horrible. When Alan Shearer wasn't playing I was given the captain's armband. What was embarrassing was when Alan, the normal skipper, was out of the side, Gullit would always ask me: "What does my captain think?" It was obviously a snipe at Alan, who didn't deserve anything like that. Alan was and still is a very good mate and I was uncomfortable with all that. Things like this didn't split the dressing room because we all got on well but it still created a bad atmosphere. I felt sorry for Alan and Rob.

Even so, like Kenny, Ruud took us to an FA Cup final. We were back at Wembley just 12 months after our defeat against Arsenal and this time it was Manchester United who were our opponents. We were confident, especially after beating Spurs 2-0 in the semi-final at Old Trafford. I thought we were good enough to win, even though United were the Premier League champions and would go on to land the Champions League.

I ended up upsetting Roy Keane. I tackled him and he injured his ankle so badly that he had to go off. It was a fair challenge and his ankle had been a bit suspect in any case. The referee was right on the spot and didn't award a free-kick so my conscience is clear. I spoke to Roy after the game and he seemed fine. He was out of the Champions League final anyway through suspension so there was no issue there but since then he has had a right go at me in his autobiography, insisting it had been a dangerous challenge and I had done him. He said I had been a "c**t". He's wrong. It was a decent tackle. I suppose Roy is the sort of character who always wants to get one over you – and most of the time he did.

With Roy off I definitely thought we would go on to win the Cup but Teddy Sheringham came on in Roy's place and scored almost straightaway. That quickly put paid to those thoughts. To be honest, although we had a couple of chances, it was one-way traffic towards our goal and they grabbed another. Another 2-0 FA Cup final defeat. This time I was devastated and it was a bad Saturday night. We all went out for a meal, had a few drinks but it was an early night. No-one felt like celebrating.

A few months later Ruud was gone. It's strange Newcastle seem to have a penchant for sacking their managers in August. It was a bad start to the season. Alan Shearer was sent off against Aston Villa, a ridiculous decision by Uriah Rennie. We lost that game and then lost our next two away matches at Spurs and Southampton, and when we drew 3-3 against Wimbledon at St. James' Park the pressure was really on Ruud. Alan had been suspended for that game but everyone thought he would be back for the next crucial match, the home derby game against Sunderland. Instead, Alan and Duncan Ferguson were left on the bench and we lost 2-1. The parting of the ways between Ruud and Newcastle was now inevitable.

Under Gullit there had been splits in the camp and five or six players, including Rob Lee, had been completely bombed out. But within a matter of days, Bobby Robson's appointment as manager changed all that. It is indeed phenomenal what Bobby was able to do in such a short period of time. In his first game we lost 1-0 against Chelsea but it was a much-improved performance. He quickly rounded us all up for a team meeting and insisted we were all in it together and that everyone would be given a fair crack of the whip. Suddenly, we all felt together. We were one happy band again, eager to play for him.

The next game was at home to Sheffield Wednesday. It was a clash between the two bottom teams. What a day. We thrashed them 8-0, Alan scored five and I got one. The amazing transition in our fortunes wasn't down to coaching or revolutionary tactics, it was simply down to fantastic man-management. Bobby is one of those guys who was charismatic, very infectious. Everyone likes him because he is a great bloke. Maybe he wasn't too hot on names and we'd all have a laugh at that. We never laughed at him – we laughed with him. One of our strikers, Shola Ameobi, was asked about nicknames and whether Bobby had one for him. "No," answered Shola, "Bobby calls me Carl Cort." Carl was another black striker at the club.

Any relegation worries were soon forgotten. We even reached the FA Cup semi-final and should have reached another final. We battered Chelsea, only to lose unluckily, but our feel-good factor amongst the players and the fans, who also loved Bobby, was the real winner.

It was a really enjoyable time, although not without a few incidents because the dressing room was full of interesting characters. Alan was the joker, always messing around, which might surprise some people. He was a good captain, very serious when it came around to winning football matches but he enjoyed off-field pranks. His finishing in training was unbelievable. He wasn't the best trainer you have ever seen but it didn't matter when it came to putting the ball in the back of the net. There were none better. He loves Newcastle and the fans and I know he has never had any regrets about turning down Manchester United in favour of playing in front of his own people every week.

How Gullit could have left big Dunc out I don't know. On his day he was an unbelievable player. Despite his size – about 6ft 5in – he was good on the ground. He was hard as nails as well. There was a spell when Dunc partnered Alan up front during Bobby Robson's time. They were both on fire. It must have been a relief for Alan to have Duncan alongside him. He had been used to going in where it hurt. Now he could leave that sort of thing to his partner in crime. Duncan was someone you would certainly have in the trenches with you. I don't think burglars were too keen on him either!

I remember him coming on during a Champions League game against Roma at St. James' Park. We had lost 1-0 in Italy and it was 0-0 at our place with about 20 minutes to go when Duncan was introduced to the game. He had been out injured for three months and had been like a bear with a sore head on the sidelines. He just lost it when he came on, mixing it with the Italians, obviously making up for lost time and scrapping with everyone.

Shay Given was a fantastic goalkeeper. I would rate him and Everton's Neville Southall as the best keepers I have played alongside. I don't think Shay has received the amount of praise he was due. Newcastle would have been relegated long before they were if it hadn't have been for Shay's heroics. He has been some signing for Manchester City. In training he is unbelievable, pushing himself to improve all the time. He's also a funny lad and one of my best mates in the game.

I believe the team spirit and camaraderie was one of the main reasons Newcastle, under Bobby Robson, created history in the Champions League – the first team to qualify from their group despite losing the first three games. It was Craig Bellamy who scored the all-important winner away at Feyenoord to seal our passage into the knockout stages.

You could see what Bobby meant to the football world through the reaction to his sad death. Any player under Bobby would run through a brick wall for him. The tributes and the outpouring of grief following his final surrender to cancer said it all. He was the tops and I'm just glad to have been able to play under him. Hopefully some of his influence will rub off on me in future years.

Talking of characters, Bellamy was one all right. Of course I knew what to expect from my days playing for Wales when he arrived. He has never been everyone's cup of tea because he says what he thinks, whether he is right or wrong, and I quite like that trait in people. He and Alan Shearer will never be bosom friends. They fell out a lot on the training ground. As I have mentioned, Alan wasn't the best trainer while Bells was – and didn't he let Alan know it. Even if Alan had been Pele or Maradona, Bells would still have let him have it with his stinging verbals. He would just go up to him and bait him, telling him he wasn't very good. It just made you cringe. The only reason they didn't come to blows on the training ground was because Alan could never catch Bells.

I lost count of the number of times I had to dive in to get Bells out of scrapes. The biggest incident happened at Newcastle Airport when we were flying off for a Champions League game. Bells, as usual, was lippy and he was having a go at the coach John Carver. John snapped and gave Craig a clip. A few of us stepped in to break things up. We moved away again and suddenly Bells picked up a chair in the airport lounge and threw it at John. Luckily, the manager wasn't there and the pair quickly made up. In fact, I know they are good mates and talk on the phone a lot.

The biggest disappointment was that Jonathan Woodgate stood up and said what had happened at the airport must stay in-house. The media mustn't get hold of the story. It was in some of the papers the next day. Obviously one of our group couldn't keep his mouth shut.

The good thing about most players is that there may be dust-ups but minutes later they are forgotten. One of the best examples of that during my time at Newcastle was a training ground fracas between the French winger Laurent Robert and hard-as-nails defender Andy Griffin. One day Griff went right through Laurent in a training game. Before Griff got up, Laurent elbowed him and Griff responded by smashing Laurent to the ground. Because Griff is so small, I think this was the last thing Laurent had expected. A few hours later we had to board the coach to travel to an away game and there they were sitting side by side, Griff with a bag of ice nursing a damaged hand and Laurent with his ice-pack over a black eye!

Even Alan got in on the act on a club trip to Ireland. Our winger Keith Gillespie had a few drinks on board and was upsetting people in a bar. It was mid-season and we were having a break. The last thing you wanted was to upset the punters. Alan decided to apologise to a few people over Keith's behaviour. Keith objected and so it went off between the two of them. They decided to go outside and before anyone knew it Keith cuffed Alan on the back of the head. That was it. Back came Alan and after one punch it was all over. Keith was lying poleaxed on the ground. Fight over.

It was a great time for me at Newcastle but sadly it ended unpleasantly. We were in Hong Kong on a pre-season tour when I received a phone call from my agent saying Newcastle had accepted offers for me from Bolton and Fulham. It was a shock because I had grown up in football believing that decisions like that were always made by the manager, who would then tell you. Now I was left with the impression the club, including Bobby Robson, didn't want me anymore. We were due to play a game and I pulled John Carver and told him I wouldn't be playing because I was about to be sold. He said he knew nothing about it and neither did Bobby. I understand Bobby was so annoyed he had a row with the chairman Freddy Shepherd in the foyer of the hotel we were staying in. Later, I asked Bobby whether he wanted me to go and he said no, he didn't. I said I had a year left on my contract and so, if that was the case, would he extend it? He said he couldn't because the chairman wouldn't allow it.

I then went to see Freddy Shepherd, who was very upfront with everything. He said he was bringing in Nicky Butt from Manchester United. I told him I was better than Nicky Butt. Looking back now, I should have stayed because I had that year left on my contract. At the time I feared I would end up on the bench with Nicky coming in and, at the age of 34, I couldn't face that prospect. I knew I was going to a smaller club in Bolton, who I agreed to join, but at least I was wanted there, unlike Newcastle.

7

PICKING UP
THE PIECES

*'I don't think Gary would have been able to express
a weakness to me. He was the one everyone else
would go to. He was the problem-solver. He would
be the strong character. That then probably makes it
even harder to admit your own weaknesses'*

O bviously the morning that it all happened will
never leave me. It was horrific. The evening before,
we had been out locally to a friend's house for a
really fun event. They had got chefs in. There were eight of
us there and we had a great laugh around the swimming
pool. It was the first night we had allowed our boys
to stay at home with their friends while Gary and I went
out. We felt they had got to that age where they could be
left. And in any case we were just up the road if there were
any problems.

The next morning back at our home turned into a horror film – something I don't really want to revisit to be honest. As time goes on you hope it's a film that fades. I try to pop that part away. It was horrific. There is no other way to describe it.

I can probably never forgive Gary for putting us all through that and everything after that. We were the ones who had to pick up the pieces. It's quite grotesque what he did to himself, I have to say that. I was the one who found him, the one who cut him down. As I say, it's just like a horror film.

I got Ed up and unfortunately he saw what his dad had done. I had to use his phone because mine wasn't charged. I made the phone call to the emergency services. Really, I just didn't know what to do. I cut him down. I was screaming at the paramedics to resuscitate him. But I knew really that he was gone. I was just screaming in hope and desperation.

I was standing in the garage where he had hung himself, shaking. One of the paramedics said to me to go inside the house and call my parents. I'd become like a little child, not knowing what to do. I then called my mum and dad and then Gary's mum and dad. I just said it as it was and it was just horrible hearing their screams of anguish on the other end of the phone.

All four of them eventually came over, some family and friends then started arriving. It was simply horrendous after that. It was on the news all day. The TV was on but I wasn't really watching it. It was like I was watching something else. That the house they were showing wasn't really ours. I wasn't really absorbing anything.

I just remember lying on the couch most of the day while

people were coming and going. A policeman came along, explained a few things and then turned to one of my friends and said I was in shock. I wasn't responding to anything. In any case, no-one really knew what to say or do.

I was so thankful I had a fantastic friend, Tracey. She was the wife of one of Gary's friends and after moving to Chester we had clicked straightaway. We started going to the gym together, loved socialising together. We have the same sense of humour and just bounce off one another.

Tracey, along with her husband Keith, had hosted the party the night before Gary ended his life.

You quickly realise the friendship you have following a tragedy. Tracey has been a rock to me. In the aftermath of Gary's death she would force me to eat in the mornings. At first I couldn't eat, the thought of food made me feel sick. I had to have food forced down me. I lost so much weight I looked like a walking skeleton. But Tracey made me eat. She forced me to go on dog walks. Really, it was Tracey who integrated me back into society.

I was lucky to have some great neighbours, John and Sarah, who also became great rocks. Their home became mine. I think I went there every night at the beginning. I just wanted to move in and be cared for – in fact I practically did. I was helped by fantastic company and some alcohol! They also taught me how to swear...

In the first 12 months, lots of people wanted to help and be around me, to try and keep me busy. Nothing was too much for them. Shay and Jane Given would turn up with food for us. Shay played football with the boys while Jane sat with me. Craig Bellamy would suddenly turn up, making sure the boys were okay. Alan Shearer's wife Lainya often arrived. Old school friends from Hawarden were there for me and I would sometimes go to stay with them at their homes.

My good friend Gill, from Newcastle, came down whenever she could in the first few months and stayed over. I just couldn't bear to be on my own at night. That went on for around the first two years.

I have to admit that I did start to drink an awful lot. I didn't need a drink as soon as I woke up but I did drink virtually every evening for the first two years. It was always wine and I felt it helped numb the pain I was suffering. For a few hours it helped make me forget the terrible event. And I know this may sound unusual but just recovering the next day brought some normality, in a bizarre way, back into my life. I felt human – it's what everyone goes through if they have had a heavy night of drinking.

Eventually I knew I had to stop drinking so much and now I just drink socially and I'm completely in control.

Gary died in the November and I didn't go out properly until the March with Tracey. She took me to a friend's house party. I really didn't feel right putting on a dress and going out. I found it hard. I was Louise Speed, wife of Gary Speed who had hung himself. How could you act normally? It was so hard. People though, generally, were very good. I think at first they approached me delicately and mindfully. I was okay as long as no-one talked about Gary. I just wanted to talk about anything but Gary.

But poignantly, when we arrived at the party the first song we heard was *Don't You Forget About Me* by Simple Minds. That was mine and Gary's song. It obviously hadn't been arranged, it just came on. It was like it was meant to be – was it a sign? To be honest it really spooked me out.

Another thing which was really poignant was I ended up registering his death exactly 12 months to the day that he managed Wales against England, which as I explained was one of his proudest moments in football.

At home I had a wall in the kitchen where everyone who came into the house had to write an inspirational quote. I would supply the black marker pen and they had to come up with the quote. That was the entry fee to my home! It was just a tiny part in the process of my healing. Little things like that really helped me. I called it my wonder wall – nothing to do with Oasis – and it was fantastic reading what had been written.

I haven't got the answers as to why he is no longer here. I can only now put it down to a mental illness. It's now coming up to seven years and you can reflect but also learn a lot more about mental instability because it's out there a lot more now. Maybe it was something Gary lived with all his life, especially after re-reading some of his early letters. He was able, perhaps, to control it by being so in control of his life. Throwing him into his football, his family – into everything.

Quite often he would take himself into a room with his guitar as a release. Football would be on the TV all the time. He lived and breathed it. He would watch all the old games as well as what was going on in the present. He had to watch every single game. He said it was his homework.

His escapism was going into a room and strumming his guitar. He had learned to play the acoustic guitar. I think one day he and Chris Coleman, his big mate in the Wales side, went out and bought guitars when they were away with the Welsh squad. They both decided they wanted to take up guitar playing.

My brother Tim, who had learned to play, would go through some Oasis songs with Gary because he was really into Oasis. Gary loved almost all music. He ended up having loads of music books, songs from The Beatles, bits of Dire Straits, a wide selection really. Sometimes, to be honest, it got on my nerves because I had to listen to him practising when his playing wasn't the best. But he stuck at it and when anyone came around to the house and we were having a night in, inevitably the guitar would come out. I used to roll my eyes!

Deep down though it didn't bother me because I knew it was his release from non-stop football. He would also take the dogs for a walk by the river in Chester as another release. Sometimes I would go with him and we would chat away about different things.

He must have felt low at different times but it was probably part of his make-up, the way he was built. Quite often, I would ask him what was wrong and he would reply that he was just tired. So really that meant he didn't have to answer. Looking back now, I do wonder if it was something else. Maybe saying he was tired was masking some things? I'm not sure. But blokes don't talk, do they?

Gary couldn't understand that people who have everything can still suffer from depression. So I don't think he would have associated anything like that about himself – that he also could have had an illness. If you've got a scar, you can see it. You can see lots of illnesses but mental illness can remain hidden – even from the person himself or herself.

As I say, maybe there was something within Gary for most of his life but he was able to move on from it most of the time. There would be something else to occupy his mind and then something else allowing him to run away or at least mask the reality. I think the adrenaline of football helped in this.

I don't think Gary would have been able to express a weakness to me. He was the one everyone else would go to. As a manager he was the one who sorted things out for others. He was the problem-solver. He would be the strong character. That then probably makes it even harder to admit your own weaknesses.

The shock is still with me today. There is not a day that goes by where I'm not in disbelief or shocked at some point of the day. Of course you have to carry on with life. You have to find a way. I had to focus on the two lads. I had their futures to look after. I've done my best. To see them now just gives me inspiration.

8

WITHOUT ANSWERS

Shay Given

Played with Gary at Newcastle, joining him on regular summer holidays to Portugal

I was in my hotel room preparing for Aston Villa's game at Swansea on the Sunday afternoon when I received a phone call from Alan Shearer. I was getting showered and freshened up ready to go down for the team meeting. I wondered what was this all about because he wouldn't usually ring on a matchday, not when you were all set to play, so I immediately thought, 'This isn't good.' It definitely wasn't. He told me that Speedo had hung himself. I remember uttering "Are you taking the piss?" because your head is in a whirl – you can't really take in what you've just been told.

Alan told me his best mate had just delivered the shocking news to him – and that he couldn't believe it but it was true. I was now in major shock. It was like a bad dream, you wonder if this is really happening. We spoke for a few more minutes but both of us were numb with shock.

I got my stuff together in the room and then went down and found the manager Alex McLeish before the team meeting was due to take place. I told him what I had heard and again, obviously, he was shocked by what had happened. The news then filtered around the players, which made it a really sombre atmosphere, but we still had to go ahead with the meeting because we had a game to play. I spoke with Craig Bellamy, who was also close to Speedo. He was again in shock, stunned by the news.

Nothing was said about me being pulled out of the game even though everyone could see how the tragic news was affecting me, Speedo and I being big friends. I was thinking to myself, 'What would he want me to do in these circumstances?' He would have wanted me to play, I was absolutely certain of that. I could almost hear him saying: "Don't be stupid, play." I thought, 'Right, I'll have to get my game head on and try and focus on the meeting.' If I'm being honest it was all a bit of a blur. I couldn't really take anything in. All that was in my mind was Speedo, his two boys, his wife Louise, his dad Roger, who I also knew quite well. I was thinking, 'Oh my god, has this really happened?'

As we made our way onto the coach which was taking us to the stadium, there was talk of the game being called off. I think it would have been a relief if it had been but we were informed it was going ahead. So it was surreal, sitting in the changing room trying to look at the match programme, which is one of the things you would normally do, but not really taking anything in.

I was just trying to keep myself together because fans were coming into the stadium and I had a job to do. It was a bit of a surprise that the game was allowed to go on because Gary Speed was the Wales manager and the game was being staged in the country. In hindsight I think the powers that be should have called it off. The atmosphere was sullen throughout the game. You imagine most people in the Liberty Stadium were talking about what had happened to Speedo.

But once we left the changing rooms I warmed up as normal. The club doctor had asked me if I was all right. I told him I was okay but I quickly realised I wasn't. We were all lined up ready for the minute's silence and when the guy on the Tannoy started talking about Gary it was suddenly so real – he wasn't with us anymore. That really hit me and I couldn't keep it together any longer. I just broke down. I was positioned in between Richard Dunne and James Collins and they were having to hold me up.

I didn't even realise the cameras were on me – they were the last thing on my mind. I was just completely lost in the emotion of it all. After all, he had only passed away a few hours earlier. Everything was still so raw. I hadn't cried in the room, in the meeting or on the bus but now it was all coming out. I'm not a big crier but all the memories about Speedo had got to me. The more the guy was talking about him, the greater the memories of him were whirling around inside my head. The place then fell silent. It was so tough, really tough.

It was no surprise there were few incidents in a goalless draw.

It was a bit of a weird game really. At least Speedo would have been pleased that I'd managed to keep a clean sheet! It was then onto the coach for the journey home, which was horrendous, with more news coming out about Speedo plus all the social media chat about him. It was still hard to believe.

He was 42 when he died. I'm 42 now, which makes it even more poignant. I'm the same age he was when he decided to end his life. I feel I've got so much more to live for over the coming years but, for reasons we will never know, he didn't feel the same.

I was one of the pallbearers at the funeral – a day which obviously brought it home to you the enormity of what had occurred. There were some fantastic readings. Alan Shearer spoke well, for instance. It was again a real struggle to keep it together listening to the wonderful eulogies for Speedo. I just felt he should have been sitting next to me rather than lying in the coffin we had just carried into the church.

Life can be cruel at times. I lost my mum to cancer when I was just four and last year a big mate of mine died when he was just 41 and left behind a four-year-old and a two-year-old. At a dinner to honour me in Donegal, I dedicated the night to him. His family were there and when I started talking about him I broke down. It was really emotional – the same as it was on that day in North Wales when we said our farewells to Speedo.

I was feeling horrendous but you're also thinking about Louise, Tom and Ed – how the hell are they getting through it? What are Roger and Carol going through? His sister? Forget all the football stuff, this is their dad, this is their son. There was the big public side because he was so well known but then there is the private side, the close family which comes with much more emotion.

Tom and Ed were not even into their teenage years when they lost a dad who they doted on.

I met them in Dubai earlier in the year, the three of us coincidently being there at the same time. They have obviously grown up and are men now, both looking like two male models. I met them at a waterpark and we had a bit of craic. They have inherited the Speed good looks. They were chiselled and everything. I think I had to put my T-shirt back on!

They have been so brave just getting on with their lives. It's good that both of them are very ambitious. I just wish Gary could be here to see it all because he would be very proud of them. When he was alive he couldn't do enough for them, taking them here, there, everywhere. So why? No-one will have the answers to the big question.

You can imagine all this has continually gone through the boys' heads because they knew how much Gary loved them. I think when something like this happens you naturally question yourself. Could I have done more? Could I have done this? Could I have done that? Could I have gone to see him more often? No-one knows if that had made any difference. But everyone is busy in their own lives. Most people's lives are hectic. He was himself. He was Wales manager and had his other commitments. It wasn't as if he was struggling in the job either – not that would be a reason for committing suicide. But everything seemed to be on the up.

We hadn't been out too often in the later years. Before we would go out lots of times. We always used to go to Alan Shearer's place in Portugal every summer. We'd have great craic. I would look after him and he would look after me. We would have great times together. But things change in life and you become busy and engrossed in your own lives.

But I met him a few months before he died. I bumped into him when he was shopping in Manchester. It was as if we were still at the same club and had been training together that morning. Straightaway there was a natural connection, asking each other how it was going etc. We would quickly end up laughing. His laugh was infectious – it would make me laugh. He had this funny squeak which would set me off. Everything seemed fine with him. That was the last time I saw him face to face. But as we all know he was on Football Focus the day before he died.

I think often when these tragedies happen the people around the person always say they can't understand it happening – that person is the last one they could imagine it happening to. It was the same with Speedo because he had so much to live for, privately with a wonderful family and a professional life which was on the rise. His playing days were over but his next chapter was very much on the up. I don't have the answer.

For Wales, I know that Chris Coleman would acknowledge the work Speedo put in which went some way to the success they enjoyed at the European Championship in 2016.

Going back to the first time I met him. I was at Newcastle United and he was the captain of Everton. I would always come out onto the pitch second behind the captain, which was usually Alan Shearer. We were playing Everton at Goodison Park and the tunnel is a bit tight there. Speedo was speaking to Alan and he then turned to me and said, "Shay, how is it going?" or something like that. I couldn't remember an opposition captain doing that so I thought to myself that was pretty good.

He later joined Newcastle and we quickly built up a good friendship. He was fantastic in the dressing room, with real leadership qualities. Alan was still captain but Gary soon became vice-captain. If things weren't right he would say something and try to change what was bothering him. If people were late or weren't doing what they should be doing, he wasn't slow to express his opinion.

We played Portsmouth at Fratton Park and Lomana LuaLua scored in the last minute against us – and he was our player! We had been 1-0 up with just 60 seconds to go, having put in a real shift against a Portsmouth side who were going well in the Premier League at the time. We had loaned LuaLua to Pompey and in those days there was no rule saying a loan player couldn't face his parent club.

Bobby Robson was the Newcastle manager. We went back to the changing room and Speedo threw the massage table which had sports drinks on it into the air. They were flying everywhere with Speedo shouting "f******g joke" and asking how the hell he was allowed to play. He was blaming the people in the boardroom who had allowed this to happen. We'd just lost two points thanks to our own player. It showed what it meant to him. I think the next season they changed the rule about loan players being able to face their own club. That though came too late for Speedo. He had gone bananas and quite rightly.

It's often said that players don't care. They earn big money and that cushions them from any raw emotions. Well here was the evidence that theory is completely wrong, certainly in Speedo's case. He was so professional in everything as a player, super fit. Yes, he liked a couple of pints or whatever, but only when the time was right. He was always one of the fittest players I've ever played with. He was always prepared to learn more ways of trying to remain at the peak of his physical game. I know when he went to Bolton he discovered more through the manager Sam Allardyce's work with the sports science side of the game. He was always open to new ideas. He was desperate to keep playing as long as he could and that was all credit to him that he would try new things.

It's always a huge culture shock when you stop playing and, to be honest, I don't think we do enough to help players through the abrupt change to their lifestyle. It's amazing how many players suffer the trauma of going through a divorce shortly after they stop playing. I went through a divorce myself but I was still playing. There are added pressures, greater tensions when you change your routine drastically. You hear of players suffering from depression after their active football life is taken from them.

Don't forget that professional players are used to going training nearly every day of their footballing lives. It's not always possible to keep that going. You can't always go to the gym when you want, especially if you have young kids. The missus might have been up through the night and you're expected to be on duty the next day while she has a lie-in or something. So your plans at staying fit for that day go out of the window. That is definitely a negative side because training has been your day job for so long. Training sends out endorphins which triggers a positive response in your body. If you miss out then your body and mind are out of synch, which can lead to problems, maybe even depression. Suddenly your regimented regime has gone out of the window.

For me it went on for 25 years or so. Then one day it's gone and some ex-players are at a complete loss. I've been lucky in the fact that I've immersed myself in the media side of the game so I'm still involved in some capacity and haven't got loads of free time. But for many players, once their careers end they are in potential trouble.

I think the Professional Footballers' Association or somebody should try to do something. I've been finished as a player almost 12 months now and in that time no-one from the PFA has been in touch or maybe explain they have a department which looks after the interests of players coming to the end of their careers, one that invites you to sit down and discuss any plans for the future. Just help with a few pointers. I've found myself that it's important to keep active but it's hard for some players because there is very little else they can do. It's been football, football all their lives, the only thing they have ever known.

Many these days will be financially sound but it's not about money. At the age of 35 or whenever players finish, there's still a lot of years ahead. There's only so many people who can stay in football as a coach or a manager or go into the media. There's a large percentage of ex-players who don't do anything. So there's a massive void in their lives. Most of us, including myself, don't have any qualifications away from football. I joined Celtic when I was 16.

As I say, I feel more could be done, especially when you see all the money flooding into the Premier League.

I know Viv Anderson is part of an organisation which tries to involve ex-players. But we need more things like this. It's all right having charity golf days and other functions but I believe more should be done on a day-by-day basis. Maybe I should have rung the PFA up and asked to speak to somebody. Anyway, let's look at ways of improving the aftercare of ex-players.

It's such a contrast. One day you might be playing in front of a big crowd, with all the adulation and what comes with being a successful professional footballer, and the next it's gone. So for some people you can imagine them falling into what seems like a dark hole. At times I've felt a bit down myself because you miss that adrenalin buzz that football gives you, playing in front of 60,000, 70,000 fans. You know that is never going to come back. It's gone for ever. That can be hard to digest.

It must be the same for top musicians. I'm a big U2 fan and I've often wondered why do they keep going on the road now that they have pretty well achieved everything and are obviously getting older. But it's their life and it's what they still enjoy doing. It's why they will still go into a recording studio for days on end. What else are they going to do? At least they can still carry on. Footballers, when they get to a certain age, can't.

I have spoken with a number of ex-players who admit they have found life hard after football. Others, you imagine, don't want to talk about any problems. Possibly that was the case with Speedo. Maybe it's a man's thing – that it's not easy for us to open up.

To be fair to the PFA, maybe they have been in touch with some people but they have insisted they don't need any help, that they were all right. It's good to listen to people and not be stubborn. We can all be pig-headed at times.

Craig Bellamy

*Played alongside his friend and mentor
for the Magpies and Wales*

I'd taken a sleeping tablet on the Saturday night because Liverpool had a big game live on Sky Sports the next day against Manchester United at Anfield. It was a 4pm kick-off so I had a bit of a lie-in. When I got up I looked at my phone and discovered I had missed calls. Two were from my big mate Kieron Dyer and one from my advisor. These were people who never called me on the day of a game. I began to realise something must be wrong.

When Kieron rang for the fourth time I answered. "Have you heard about Speedo," he said. "What?" I said. "Shay's [Given] rung our agent to say Speedo's committed suicide," Kieron said. "F**k off," I said. "No chance."

"I've heard he's hung himself," Kieron replied. "F*****g no chance," I said again. "You know what Twitter and the internet are like. It's bullshit."

I got into my car to drive to Anfield. That was the routine on the day of a home match. Hop on the coach to Melwood. Do all the pre-match stuff there. Then my advisor rang me. He was ringing with the same news. He said Speedo had committed suicide. I still didn't believe it, I couldn't see it. Not with Speedo. I still thought it was bullshit. I rang Shay Given.

"It's true mate," Shay said.

When I got onto the coach I went to the back of it and rang Suzanne, who worked as a PA for both me and Speedo. I asked her if she had heard anything. "No, nothing," she said. I asked her to find out. I was starting to freak out.

I rang Speedo's phone. It started ringing. "He's alive." I thought. "Thank f**k for that."

Stupid, wasn't it? A dead man's phone can ring too. Suzanne rang back. She was hysterical. She told me it was true. I couldn't comprehend it. Speedo was my idol in football. I spoke to him pretty much once a week for the last 10 years. Then the tears started to fall. I knew it was real. I just broke down. I rang my wife and told her. She was numb with shock. She was worried about me too.

I got off the coach at Melwood and walked into the manager Kenny Dalglish's office. He was with Steve Clarke, his assistant manager.

"Look mate," Kenny said. "I don't know what to say or how to say it but I have been told that Speedo has committed suicide." I started crying. My mind was racing. Why had he done it? Everything was going so well.

"Go home," Kenny said. "Go back to Cardiff. You're not playing today."

"I want to play," I said. "I want to play through it."

"You can't play today."he said. "You're not in a fit state of mind. I'm taking the decision. Come back when you're ready."

He is always in my thoughts, especially when Wales play. Even more so when I'm coaching. I always look back and remember certain things which have been influenced by

Speedo. I wish he was here so my players could take things from him. He is the benchmark for what you would like your players to become – the way he himself as a player approached training.

Then after that how he would impart information as an ex-player to the current players. He could put things over in a way that players could understand. They would quickly take on board what he was saying.

As a player in the same dressing room, both with Wales and during our time together at Newcastle I saw this incredible work ethic in training, his will to win, a drive to do things properly. What he did, you immediately wanted to follow. If he was doing his warm-ups, you wanted to be alongside him doing the same things. Just about everything he did, you wanted to latch onto him, even trying to copy what he ate, how he looked after himself generally – how he would always take himself off to the gym after training. He was an inspiration if, as a footballer, you wanted to better yourself – as I did.

You knew that if you followed Speedo's example then you would have the best chance of staying in the game at the highest level to a fair old age. I knew if I wanted to last as long as him – and he was 10 years older than me – I had to try and sustain the same level of training and fitness that he illustrated so effectively.

That is very difficult when you are young because you don't look into the future. You think that nothing will change and that leads to doing stupid things. That's part of being young and growing up. Even he would have done some stupid things when he was growing up as a player – no-one is immune to immaturity at times – even Speedo.

When I first got to know him, when we met up for Wales games, what struck me immediately was his desire for the team to do well. He was one of our big players, amongst the elite group with the likes of Ryan Giggs and Mark Hughes. The difference was he exuded energy all the time, always ready to help the other players. He was charismatic, a good-looking bastard as well. He had just about everything going for him.

While he would pass on good advice, especially to the younger players, he wasn't afraid to have a go at anyone he felt wasn't giving their all, even if they were mates of his. That's something I always love about players, the ones who are prepared to call out their friends if things aren't going the right way. He was completely honest so if Speedo was having a go at you, you knew you had done something wrong.

He would never accept Wales losing games. We had players from all the leagues and some were just happy to be there, whereas if he turned up he was going to give everything he had. So there were no excuses. He always felt we should have been doing better than we were. If he had something to get off his chest then he would let fly, even if the manager was in attendance. I haven't seen many more vocal players in my time than Speedo.

There was a big blow-out when we were playing Tunisia. Bobby Gould was the manager and Gary was right. What had happened hadn't been acceptable. We had lost 4-0 and Bobby was telling us that Tunisia weren't a bad team so there was nothing to be ashamed about. Speedo wasn't having that – he told Gouldy in no uncertain terms that Tunisia weren't anywhere near being a good team, that England would batter them in the forthcoming World Cup game in France '98 and that Tunisia would be on the first flight home.

He said we hadn't been organised, lost possession too easily, were too easy to play against. We had played like a pub team and that Gould had set the country back years. He was spot-on and there was no real comeback from Bobby. He knew, we all knew, that when Speedo spoke he really meant what he was saying.

It was never for effect. He was doing it for the benefit of everyone. This hadn't been a calculated assassination of Bobby and his tactics. It wasn't personal. Wales meant so much to him. It was also in June when some players had pulled out, making excuses that they couldn't make the trip. He was there. He had made the effort but was now completely embarrassed by our display.

It had been shocking all round. We even had to change hotels because our original one wasn't up to standard. Again it was Speedo who had insisted the players weren't going to put up with the original base. The lack of organisation surrounding an international team had got to him and the abject display was the last straw. He didn't accept the amateur nature of Wales at that time – something he would help change later as a manager.

I was just around 18 at that time so things like hotels and organisation didn't really bother me but, with Speedo around, you quickly learned not to accept second best.

You get loads of players at clubs who keep their mouths shut, never saying anything, but they have a lot to say behind people's backs. A lot to say. Speedo was definitely not like that at all. If he had something to say, he would say it. He was no goodie-goodie. He had a temper on him. If you saw any signs of that erupting you shut up pretty quickly.

At Newcastle he was the leader in the changing room. He was the boss, someone you wouldn't answer back to. He would be vocal at training, not just around matches. You might mumble under your breath if he was having a go but you knew deep down he was right. Good players know if they're not pulling their weight. He expected everyone to put in the same effort as him.

It meant that younger players like myself and Kieron Dyer were driven to greater heights in training just following his example. It was done for your benefit as well as that of the team.

I know at times I could be a bit of a handful but that never bothered Speedo. He seemed to look out for me because he witnessed how hard I trained. There was never any need to have a moan at me and if I moaned about another player he knew I was right. He had me every day working at 100mph.

I'm like that now as a coach. Yes, this player may annoy you at times but does he give his all? Does he do the best he can to try and make himself the best he could be? If that's the case then I don't have a real problem. Maybe that's why I had such a good relationship with him because he could see my desire and determination to be the best I could be. I didn't know how long I was going to be in football so I was always prepared to go all out for as long as I could.

Sometimes I couldn't sleep the night before because I would be excited, looking forward to the training session the next day. In many ways that was the same mentality that Speedo possessed. There was a connection straightaway.

As far as his nutritional habits went, I was already looking after myself in that direction. I had learned quite a lot on that score during my time at Norwich. It was passed on to me at Norwich from a young age, eating well, drinking the right fluids.

When he was doing it as a young player at Leeds, it was a different era when things like that weren't at the fore of the game. I noticed at Newcastle and with Wales he was fully on top of all that.

You could see he was almost certain to make a good coach and manager because of his leadership qualities. I became more of a leader in my later years. I'm still not a massive leader but Speedo was born to lead. That's a very rare quality. Someone like Roy Keane, for instance, is simply born that way. I think it often depends on what position you play in the team on how you can effect the game. As a midfielder, which Speedo was, you can certainly do that. I imagine he was always the captain no matter what the age group. They are born to take a group and lead from the front.

The rest of us, myself included, we learn from that. You take it on board and maybe grow into leadership later on. Without someone like Speedo you would get nowhere near being able to lead.

So why isn't he here now, having illustrated all those qualities of leadership? I couldn't tell you. I don't ever really go into it because that's more for his family. I just know the impact he has had on my life has been huge. He has influenced me, changed me in many respects. I am grateful for that. Like everyone else I would have wanted more, much more of his time.

I look back and wonder whether I would have played longer

if he had continued as Wales manager. Would I have later been part of his backroom coaching staff? You look at that kind of stuff. You just never know. At least I did get to know him well and so you can't be greedy.

It was also nice getting to know his two lads, Ed and Tommy, and I still keep an eye out for them. They have been brilliant. It's been a great move for them going to the USA. It's an educational experience of a lifetime. They are good boys. They have their own lives to lead but the core values that Speedo brought to the home, the discipline, will stand them in good stead even though at times it will be hard to live up to. I am sure when they get older and become fathers themselves – and I'm certain to an extent they think that now – they will realise how important he was.

They have both inherited the Speed good looks. With Gary and Louise as parents they were always going to do all right.

They both did brilliantly to lead out Wales in the tribute game, against Costa Rica, in Cardiff just a few months after their father's death. I stood next to them. They were incredibly brave. It was a surreal evening thinking about the last time Wales had played with Gary as manager – and now without him. It was still too raw for me. Not just in football but in life in general, things move on.

As a squad of fairly young players I always felt they were going to move on and qualify for a major tournament, which of course they did – reaching the semi-finals of the 2016 European Championships.

From a selfish aspect, I always believed we would have qualified for the World Cup finals in Brazil in 2014 if Gary had still been manager. I was pinning everything on being there. His death, I felt, changed all that and we didn't make it. Who wouldn't have wanted to play in a World Cup, especially in Brazil? So that was an incredible disappointment.

His passing has made me look more closely at myself as a person. When something tragic like this happens I think we all have to seek a reality check. As I've said, we will never explain his departure. It's made me more aware of how vulnerable we all can be.

For instance, when you finish playing football – something you have done all your life – it's a very different world out there. I'm just glad I'm still involved, working with youngsters at Cardiff City. It has helped give me the fun side of life again. I purposely didn't go into a high-pressure situation of being a Football League manager straightaway. I didn't want to put myself into that position because the stress levels automatically go up.

I wanted that easier period of learning the coaching side and to have some fun again, to relax. In my job I'm not judged by results. It's about improving young players. That all changes when you take on the big managerial jobs – it's a whole new mindset. It's then when results consume everything else.

As a person, Speedo's death begs the question: Am I the person I want to be? Am I too ruthless, too nice or too generous out there? I think I've taken a conscious look at everything. I know I've still not got everything right but someone's sudden departure makes you try and spend more time with the people you love, like and trust.

You never know what is around the corner, in football or in life. Next week something can happen that you could never see coming. In football, more often than not, it's the sack as a manager! The game is so complex. It's so up and down but that's the fascination of it as well. It's my adrenaline. It's often exciting living on the edge but sadly people can fall off it.

Steve Harper

One of Gary's regular holiday companions, he struggled with depression while playing for Newcastle

My eldest son James was playing rugby on the Sunday morning and I was sat there watching with a couple of mothers watching their lads. Alan Shearer rang me and he just said: "Harps, Speedo is dead, I'll phone you back." He just hung up. Obviously he was in shock. I'm now desperately trying to ring him back. I'm in utter disbelief searching for answers. I had to walk away from the other parents so as to try and find out what was going on with Speedo.

I finally managed to get hold of Alan, who told me briefly what had happened. I walked past everyone at the game to the far end, where there were some trees, in complete shock. Then friends started texting me asking if I'd heard the shocking news. Was it true? All this sort of stuff.

Alan Shearer and his wife Lainya lived across the road and that night they came over to my house. We had a few drinks and just talked, trying to get our heads around what had happened. We were all sat around, in complete disbelief. I was looking at my phone and seeing Speedo's number – a number you knew you would never ring again. There's no manual to help you deal with something that happens like this. That whole day, to be honest, is a bit of a blur.

But there were some great times with Speedo, none more so than the times we spent in Portugal. Every year we would go off to Alan Shearer's place there for a week to play golf. I roomed with Gary during these annual trips. I think we went seven years running. Speedo always left me in charge of the air conditioning so the room would no doubt be absolutely freezing when we got back at 2am or 3am. After a good few drinks, you needed that.

It was great that we could let our hair down after a tough season. There was plenty of golf played – even if there were sometimes a few sore heads. The first year we went we sometimes played twice in one day. It became a marathon so, in the following years, we just played once a day. Also, the golf was put back until around lunchtime, allowing us to pull ourselves around from the previous night.

Eight of us would always go and we'd have games against people who were also in Portugal. We'd have doubles games and the losers would pay for the meals that night. We'd also have games of singles with the losers paying again for the food. It was great craic.

We'd end up putting the world to rights sitting on the balcony of Alan's villa. After working hard for 10 months you needed a break like this. Alan, Speedo and Shay Given were great professionals who gave their all day in, day out, and were perfectly entitled to enjoy a few games of golf and some good nights out. They were special, special times.

As a golfer, Speedo was very competitive. Typical of him as well, he had a beautiful golf swing. He always looked immaculate, he looked a million dollars. He was never tentative if the pressure was on. He would, for instance, belt in his short putts. There was no hesitation, he went for it. He was always so positive and aggressive, meaning he rarely failed with those two, three, four-footers.

One day his short game did go but the next day he got up determined to put it right and nailed it. That is the ultimate sportsman, the ultimate competitor at work.

A few times myself, Alan, Gary and some other friends from the Ponteland area, near Newcastle, would head down to Saint-Tropez and spend three or four nights there. We'd go around to some fantastic restaurants. One evening, we went into this restaurant but weren't happy with the table we had been allocated. We could see the best table in the house which was very central and so asked, how about that one? The guy hinted that if you had that table you were expected to spend an awful lot of money. We liked to have a good time but we were sensible.

We decided to sit down at this table. Maybe we had been recognised and they thought, being footballers, this was going to turn into a big-hitters' table – money no object. A waiter appeared and plonked down this huge bottle of champagne. You're a bit giddy, the sun's shining. It's full of good-looking people having a good time. When this bottle arrived I think myself, Alan and Steve Bruce, who was with us, said yeah, fine.

We're just about to open it when Speedo goes: "Hey wait a bit, hang on." He's seen the menu and spotted that this bottle is 10,000 euros! We had just been about to pop the cork and so it was a lucky escape as we sent it back. Luckily, he had his wits about him otherwise I'd still be there now washing the dishes.

He also came to the rescue at my wedding. I got married in 2002 in Edinburgh. My wife Lynsey is Scottish and we had the reception at the golf place, Dalmahoy. I'd gone for a Beatles tribute band which would have got everyone bouncing but my father-in-law Douglas insisted that we left the band to him. He said he knew just the band who were always booked up years in advance and they would be brilliant. Not to worry.

Our wedding song for some reason was *Tonight I Celebrate My Love For You*. It's music for a slow, beautiful first dance which you are a bag of nerves for. Lynsey and I got up to dance but the woman singer absolutely murdered it, so much that it went from cringeworthy to comical. We let it go for a few songs and then it got painful so we had to get rid.

The night before, Speedo had got his guitar out among a few of us, the lads and dads etc, and played a few tunes for us to sing along to. So he went up to his room, retrieved his guitar and took over and saved the day, as far as the music was concerned, for our wedding. He got the place going and everyone loved it. I remember in particular he did a great version of *Get Back* by The Beatles. He did *Brown Eyed Girl* by Van Morrison, which went down well. He was very special.

When I was 30, which was in 2005, I had a spell suffering from depression. Although I didn't speak about it at the time I asked for help. People around me knew that I had sought help. Gary was one of those who knew I had been going through a bad time.

Having roomed with him, I would feel a little disappointed if something like this had contributed to his death and he hadn't confided in me. If he was suffering, I wish he had come to me and talked about it. But to be honest, he would be the last person on earth that you would think something like this would happen to. He looked like he was chiselled out of rock and appeared rocklike.

It's still hard to comprehend what occurred. Although I must admit initially I bottled up what I was going through. At first you don't understand it. You're proud. You try and fight it yourself. I was fortunate that eventually I was able to turn to some friends and get help.

There were good people at the football club, Newcastle United. The medical staff were very helpful. Once I opened up, I went independently to a little old lady in her house. As soon as you start talking, things are placed into perspective and things make more sense. It makes it easier to get through. Being able to open up is a strength. It's a real strength.

I've recently finished a Masters Degree in Sporting Directorship and the dissertation was on VAR – so it wrote itself! So I'm doing fine now.

Terry McDermott

Helped sign Gary for Newcastle, and was part of the group that went to the Algarve every summer

I was the assistant manager of Huddersfield and travelling down on the coach to a game against Charlton Athletic. I was sat at the front of the coach with the manager Lee Clark and Derek Fazackerley. I had noticed a missed call from Alan Shearer. When he rang again I went to sit on the steps of the coach next to the driver. I thought it might be important because Alan wouldn't normally call on a Sunday morning.

He asked me first if I was sitting down. I told him I was perched on the steps of the coach. He then came out with the news that Speedo was dead. I know it's a silly thing to say but I blurted out: "Stop taking the piss." But deep down I knew he wasn't messing around – not with such an awful message as this. It was just a nervous reaction to terrible news. I'm still in shock to this day, especially learning what had happened.

I went to Lee Clark and told him he wasn't going to believe it but Speedo had hung himself. He was completely dazed, hardly able to take it all in, just like I was. We broke the news to Faz, who also knew Speedo. We could hardly talk, just looking at one another in bewilderment. The news then started filtering around the coach to the players.

Eventually we were watching the event unfold on the TV and listening to things on the radio. It was a horrible journey. My stomach was churning, unable to grasp what had happened.

I imagine only Gary really knows what was going on inside his head. You can speculate and speculate about the reasons but he has taken them to his grave.

I'd only seen him around a month earlier. Lee and I had gone down to Cardiff to watch a game. We were sat in the stand and suddenly someone placed their hands over our eyes and asked, who was it? We had no idea and there was Speedo having a bit of fun as usual. He's just a great guy, always ready for a laugh.

Someone who you always loved being around. Both Lee and I were really chuffed to see him because as Wales manager we hadn't seen too much of him in recent months.

When he was at Newcastle I would see him and his wife Louise, his mum and dad regularly in the local Chinese restaurant.

I could sometimes be coming in to order a takeaway for my family and if Speedo was in there I would end up getting back to the house two hours late. He was great company and we would laugh and joke until I realised it was probably time to go home because everyone would have been starving wondering where their food was.

He was a great guy, full of charm and charisma. I've never heard anyone have a bad word against him in all the time I've been in football and that's unusual. In fact it never happens, there's always someone who doesn't like you for some reason.

Speedo had everything going for him. We would often say to him: "Hey look at you. You're a great footballer, you're bloody good-looking, you've got a beautiful wife, lovely kids, a great big fantastic house and look at the rest of us!" Everyone would swoon over him whenever he entered a room but no-one was jealous because everyone liked Speedo.

It was like royalty walking in – everyone wanted a photo with him. He always obliged. He wasn't one to say that he was out with his family and didn't want to be bothered. He would do anything willingly. He was just a genuine guy and it's still horrible thinking that he is no longer with us and searching for clues as to why he ended what had seemed such a perfect life.

Before meeting him for the first time, I knew of him, having watched him play on the TV. I knew he was a really good player. It came to the stage that when I was assistant manager to Kenny Dalglish at Newcastle, I played a part in us signing him. We used to call him Postman Pat because when we were attempting to bring him to Newcastle he kept on posting transfer requests at Everton. I'd be on the phone nearly every day talking to him because we were desperate to sign him and we knew he wanted to leave Everton. Kenny would keep asking, had I rang him that morning? I kept telling him to put in a written transfer request. Finally, Everton agreed to let him go.

I quickly discovered when he was at Newcastle that he was one of the nice guys of football. It was simple for Kenny, he wanted him in his side because he was a brilliant player. He could play as a midfielder through the middle or wide on the left. To be honest, you could have played him anywhere and he wouldn't let you down. He proved to be a fantastic player for Newcastle. It took the fans a while to take to him, probably because of his Leeds United links – Leeds were then looked at as one of the main enemies along with Sunderland.

He ended up staying at Newcastle a fair few years and ended up as a real fans' favourite. He was great to have around in the dressing room because he wanted to have his say. If he spoke then everyone listened. He wasn't someone to scream and shout or moan all the time. He reserved his opinions to when he felt they were needed. He was certainly one of the best professionals I have worked with.

He loved his social life with the lads. Despite being a superb professional he wasn't a goody-goody, a management lackey. He was definitely one of the lads who loved a good time. In football you are usually one or the other – he could be both.

Every May, following the end of the season, a group of us, including Speedo, would head off to a place Alan Shearer had in Portugal. It was always the same eight people packing our golf clubs and playing in the sunshine of the Algarve. Three of them weren't footballers, the rest were. There was Alan, Steve Harper, Shay Given, Speedo and myself. I think we went out there for seven or eight years running. We had the most unbelievable laughs in addition to alcoholic poisoning! The camaraderie was sensational.

We did manage to fit in games of golf – too many for my liking. We would play at 9am, which wasn't the best when you were suffering from an almighty hangover. Sometimes we'd only got in from a heavy night out just a few hours before. We'd always end up at a place called Montys where you could drink as long as you wanted. The only reason they ended up kicking us out would be so they could open up again for breakfast.

The fun we had was beyond belief. No-one loved that time more than Speedo. He was in his element. He loved the golf – but no more than he loved the drinking sessions. I remember one day coming in from the night out and we were sitting in the garden and suddenly Speedo, obviously a little spaced out by another heavy session, insisted that Louise, his lovely wife, was watching him from the trees in the distance. He swore she was there until he eventually came to his senses. So that was it, the next night wherever we went we would tell him: "Be careful, Louise is over there!"

Glory night: No better feeling than playing football – Gary scored 40 goals for Newcastle

Travels: In Red Square, Moscow, ahead of the first leg of Wales' Euro 2004 play-off tie against Russia

Thrill: Steven Gerrard with Gary's son Ed when he was mascot for Liverpool

Wedding singer: Enjoying a night out with Warren Barton and Louise

Side by side:
Observing a
minute's silence
at Newcastle
with Shay Given

Class acts:
Arriving at the
PFA awards
ceremony in
2003 with Alan
Shearer

All four one: With Newcastle team-mates Steve Harper and Alan Shearer as part of a
syndicate backing local golfer Gary Donnison *(far right)*

Friends and rivals: Coming up against Wales team-mate Robbie Savage during a Bolton versus Blackburn clash

Two's company: Celebrating with Kevin Nolan after scoring for Bolton against Aston Villa in 2007

Making waves: Travelling on board a boat along the River Dee with Louise to celebrate the wedding of his friend, and the author of this book, John Richardson

Stepping up: Coaching at Sheffield United opposite former Leeds team-mate and Middlesbrough manager Gordon Strachan

Proud day: Posing for the press after being unveiled as Wales manager in 2010

Role model: *(Right)* With Louise, attending a fashion charity event in Manchester in 2011, organised by friend Shay Given

Happy days: With friends, including Alan Shearer, on holiday

Raising a glass: Gary with friends, including Steve Bruce, in Saint-Tropez. Gary saved the party from buying a €10,000 bottle of champagne!

Holiday snap: Gary with Louise in the summer before he died

Alone: In a thoughtful mood ahead of his final game as Wales manager, against Norway in November 2011

Pointing the way: Instructions from the touchline during the 4–1 win over Norway in Cardiff

Put it there: Thanking Craig Bellamy for his contribution

Football family: Dad Roger with Ed and Tommy *(above left)* and alongside Gary's mum Carol and Chris Coleman *(above right)* at the Gary Speed memorial match in February 2012

Together: Louise with Tommy and Ed

Feeling good: Louise with friend Tracey after a hard run

Mystery guest: An image taken during Gary's appearance on A Question Of Sport

The sad thing is that everything seemed to be going for him before he died. Wales had picked up under him and that job would have suited him down to the ground. He was a very shrewd operator, very proud of being Welsh, and wanted to do a good job.

For whatever reason he didn't remain in the job for too long. Again you ask yourself, why Gary? Why?

As far as I was concerned there were no signs of any depression being in Speedo. He seemed so happy and more than content with everything he had. There was never a time when any of us would think, 'He's not the same fella is he?' That never, ever occurred and I'd been with him on numerous occasions. I'd been away with him for weeks at a time. Spending all that time you get to know people's characteristics. You can sense when they are the not the same – that something isn't quite right. He was exactly the same – full of fun – every time I saw him.

He would always be laughing and joking and asking about our next trip to Alan's place in the Algarve. All of us couldn't wait for May to come around – it was one of the highlights of the year.

Once Speedo left us we never repeated the golfing week. When he died a part of us died with him. It didn't seem right to try and recapture the camaraderie we had without Speedo. How could we, for instance, try to bring somebody else in to replace him? You just can't.

No-one said we were knocking it on the head. It wasn't mentioned. It just didn't happen again. Nobody had to actually say anything. I miss this week a lot. But I miss Speedo a hell of a lot more.

Bryn Law

First met Gary as a young reporter at Radio Leeds,
and a close friendship blossomed

I had taken my kids to a place in Leeds called Tropical World for a little break after working for Sky Sports' Soccer Saturday the previous day, covering Leeds United and Barnsley. During the course of the first half the phone had pinged with a text message from Gary Speed stating that the first snows of winter had fallen in West Yorkshire – a typical reference to the fact that my hair had gone white. Whenever I popped up on telly, that message would inevitably follow.

On the Sunday we were returning from a morning out looking at the various animals, butterflies, tropical plants etc in the hothouse and I was under orders to buy some margarine on the way home. So I quickly stopped at a shop having left my phone in the car. By the time I had returned there were a number of missed calls. I wondered what on earth was going on.

I rang home to say we were on our way back and my wife added to the confusion by informing me that Sky had been trying to get me on our home number. That was unusual because they never normally rang me on the home number. It would always be on the mobile. There were missed calls from them on the mobile.

I thought I'd better try and get hold of them so I rang the Sky Sports news desk and the news editor said he wanted me to check out some information they had been given, that

Gary Speed was dead. It was a pretty stark message, absolutely brutal. I don't know if he was aware I had known Gary for a long time. Anyway, there it was and somehow I had to deal with this news.

My immediate reaction was: "Well that has got to be a whole load of bollocks." It couldn't be right. Back came the reply: "That's what people are saying." I just thought it must surely be one of those daft internet rumours. I asked how he was supposed to have died. The answer was he had supposedly committed suicide.

"That's definitely bollocks then," I retorted. I told the news editor that Gary had sent me a jokey text message the previous afternoon. He insisted that I check it out because the info had come from what they regarded as a good source.

My two children were watching on from the back of the car as all this unfolded. They could see the conversation had affected me. My head was now spinning. I decided to ring Mark Evans, who worked for the Football Association of Wales, after leaving Gary a message telling him to call me back because a stupid rumour was doing the rounds. I said to Mark I was ringing him about a stupid Gary Speed story which seemed to be gathering momentum. He said sadly it was true.

It was like someone had punched me in the stomach. I was completely floored. Mark said he was drinking cup of tea after cup of tea trying to get his head around the dreadful news.

I drove home and parked up on the drive. My wife came out of the house and before I had got out of the car one of my daughters ran towards her and asked her if she had heard that Gary Speed was dead. She had also met him and knew him to an extent, so she had to take everything in as well.

I went upstairs and the rest of the day was just horrendous. The worst day of my life, without a doubt. I basically locked myself in the bedroom and couldn't stop myself sobbing. The phone was going almost constantly, people like Barry Horne just wanting to talk because they were in shock, not knowing how to handle it. In the midst of it all, Sky News were ringing me because they wanted me to cover the awful story. One of the guys said he knew I had lost a good contact but could I help them? A good contact!!! I'd known the guy 20 years. He was much, much more than a good contact. I classified him as a close mate. I'd also got to know the family over the years, especially his dad Roger. When I used to commentate on Leeds United, Roger would often walk past our positions in the stand and have a chat.

I was in bits, hardly able to think about talking about Gary to the nation on Sky. It should have been apparent to them that I was in no fit state to work. In the end I told them I would help them out the following day. So at 6.30am I found myself outside Elland Road in the dark standing next to the Billy Bremner statue. Plenty of tributes to Gary were already appearing. Simon Grayson came down to be interviewed. They had both signed for Leeds on the same day as youngsters.

For the rest of the day I reported for Sky Sports News and it was just horrendous. I was still there at 5pm and by then I was completely frazzled. It had been a gruelling experience, so hard to take in. Then there was the added pressure of attempting to be coherent on live television. In the end I simply didn't have anything left and I broke down in front of the camera.

The cameraman then rang Sky and told them they couldn't keep me there any longer, there was nothing more to give. I eventually made my way home and had the next day off. But there were still loads of phone calls. Everyone close to Gary needed to speak to somebody.

I'd first got to know him after joining Radio Leeds in 1992. I started the summer after Leeds, with Gary in the side, had just won the First Division championship. My first game was at Wembley in the Charity Shield, Leeds beat Liverpool 4-3 with Eric Cantona scoring a hat-trick, a cracking game to kick me off.

Because I was from North Wales having been brought up in Wrexham, and being a huge Wales fan, the fact Leeds had a Welsh player in Gary Speed was obviously of great interest to me. I'd be sent down to Elland Road on a Thursday to get some interviews for the weekend. I would often make a bee-line for Gary for two reasons. Firstly, he would always stop and be prepared to do something and, secondly, because he was a Welsh international and I would enjoy chatting to him about Wales. We quickly developed a good relationship.

He was one of the go-to players in that squad. A number of them were tricky to deal with – they didn't really want to know. Gary was always polite and accommodating. It was the early days of mobile phones and he was one of the first to pass on his number to me, which was fantastic and pretty unusual.

A year later, my Radio Leeds career moved on and I was handed the gig of doing all the Leeds United commentaries home and away. That meant I saw a lot more of Gary. If they lost, especially away from home, the hardest job was always to try and find a player who would stop and talk about the match. In that first side I covered, you could usually rely on

Gary along with the likes of David Wetherall. Later there were people like Lucas Radebe and Nigel Martyn.

So to have someone like Gary, a Wales international and somebody who had developed by then into a great player, was a real bonus for me.

When Gary left to go on his travels to the likes of Everton and Newcastle, I didn't see as much of him for a few years. With me still covering Leeds, our paths would only cross if he was part of the opposition side. I was still watching him in a Wales shirt, though as a fan who would travel all around Europe.

I remember bumping into Roger Speed at the airport before flying off to Helsinki to watch Wales against Finland and having a chat, arranging to go out for a drink the night before the game. Against Russia in Moscow, I went to see Wales train, which was an opportunity to talk to Gary.

We really became close again when I moved to Sky Sports and Gary joined Sheffield United, a club which was on my patch to cover. He also started doing some punditry work for Sky on Wales games. Part of my work was also covering Wales, so luckily I was dealing with him again, which was brilliant. I was now seeing him on club and country business.

He hadn't changed one bit. He was still giving me a bit of stick as part of the banter we shared.

I was there the night he made his final appearance as a player for Wales. He hadn't announced that it would be his last game and so I managed to do the interview which revealed his decision to retire as an international player.

He then moved into coaching at Sheffield United and I was also by then involved in media training for the Welsh FA. By coincidence, Gary was part of the first course I did as part of his coaching badges. My session was scheduled for the last night of an intensive two-week course – and on a Saturday, with Gary and the rest of them looking forward to a good night out. He was messaging me to make sure I kept my course short!

When he was doing the Wales games as a studio guest we spent a lot of time in Cardiff together. There were some good nights out and during them you saw at close hand the effect he had on people. I remember him walking into the bar at Hilton Hotel in the city and the whole place went quiet. You can imagine it. There he is with his film-star looks and I'm there walking in his shadow. It was as if you should be carrying his bags or something.

He didn't disappear. He was always happy to talk to people and have photos taken with him. He was always very good if you went out in a group. He made those who didn't know him feel part of everything. Nobody would be allowed to be on the periphery. Most of us would also wake up the next morning with a right hangover – the evidence of a great night out.

Gary soon became manager of Sheffield United and, shortly afterwards, Wales decided to dispense with John Toshack. I talked to people at the Welsh FA about who they were going to go for. Gary had publicly ruled himself out insisting he had a job to do at Sheffield United. Even so, I received a call from someone at the Welsh FA telling me they were interested in Gary but they didn't think it would be possible to get him.

There was some bad weather at the time and I was desperately searching around looking for something to put forward to Sky. Maybe Gary would be up for doing something, I thought. He agreed to do a piece about how difficult it is to train in the midst of winter. But he added that I must join him for a cup of tea beforehand in the canteen.

He asked me about the Wales job and added that he might, after all, be interested. So I rang someone at the Welsh FA to place them in the picture. Also, at the time Sheffield United weren't on a great run of form and maybe they were thinking about whether to make a change. As far as Wales was concerned, Gary was optimistic for the future because he felt there were a few good young players ready to burst through.

After speaking to the Welsh FA, I got the sense that it was very much Gary's job if he really wanted it. I told them the Sheffield United contract situation wouldn't represent a hurdle. So things started moving.

As a journalist, I knew I would have to use the story of Gary and Wales at some stage. The Welsh FA were okay with that but, as soon as I announced it, Sheffield United put out a statement saying this was untrue. That proved just to be part of the cut and thrust, and very quickly Wales got their man.

I knew how much he wanted it. I also knew how proud Roger and Carol, Gary's mother, would be at their son being manager of Wales. For me it was fantastic to see him there at press conferences sitting at the table in charge of the country I had always supported.

Welsh football was on its knees at that point. It was as bad as it had ever been. Nobody could see a way out. Crowds had dwindled away to almost nothing. The Toshack years had been difficult. I had been in the midst of all that covering Wales. It came to a head in what proved to be his last game in charge away to Montenegro. Craig Bellamy was the captain and he had refused to do an interview. At the end of the game I had asked Tosh about his position and he had a go at me.

The next day we were all corralled into a little airport, which wasn't great. The atmosphere was really bad. It was a five-hour flight and then I had a five-hour trip back to Yorkshire from Cardiff Airport in the car. It looked like any chance of qualifying for the next World Cup had already gone. I'd had enough and I rang Gary telling him I was thinking of retiring from covering international football. He said stick with it because things would get better – and under him they did.

As we know, he ended up getting the job. After doing my bit to help him, he asked me to come down to Cardiff because he wanted to take me out for a meal to thank me. At one point during the meal he raised a glass and toasted me, which was just fantastic and illustrated what a great guy he was.

It's things like that which separated him from other people in football. They might appear small gestures but really they were huge in human terms.

We were in close contact during the period when he was Wales manager. I would try to guide him on things which could have caused a few problems, media wise. He would give me the inside track and we would work out what to do. He was a dream to deal with on a professional basis.

The final match interview with Gary was after Wales had beaten Norway 4-1 at home. A pal of mine who had watched the interview rang me the next day and said he half expected the pair of us to burst into laughter because both of us had been buzzing at watching that display after all the hard years which had gone before. Sam Vokes had netted a couple and Gareth Bale had scored a great goal. There was a sense that something was now happening. It appeared that the excitement of what was happening came through in the interview.

There was excitement about the future. He texted me after the World Cup qualifying draw. He thought we had a chance. The future seemed so bright.

There was an incident with Aaron Ramsey being pictured on the front page of the well-read magazine Four Four Two. That would have worried the Wales fans because there was talk that if our players represented Great Britain in the Olympics it could affect the home nations continuing as they are under FIFA – that it could eventually lead to a Great Britain side.

We both decided to try and nip it in the bud so I travelled over to his house in Chester to put the record straight with a piece for Sky. Louise was there and we shared a pot of tea. Afterwards, he admitted it was the first time he had conducted an interview in his home. I was staggered by that.

He was laughing and joking about going to the hairdressers later that day and what style he should go for. Would he need botox?! That sort of knockabout stuff. We shook hands and that was that.

The next time I saw the house it was on the news following his death. There was absolutely no clue about what was going to happen to him. That comes after spending a lot of time with him – and some of it away from work.

The crazy thing is that he did everything that was expected of him on the day before his death, including sending me a daft text message. If it had been a car crash, that would have been terrible, but these things do happen fairly regularly. It's been quite emotional since because I've seen quite a lot of Roger and Carol, helping them with their charity golf days and stuff like that.

I was invited to join them when Leeds played Newcastle a couple of seasons back. I walked around the pitch with them and that was amazing. The worst aspect of this is what it leaves behind.

Incredibly, I now know three fathers in my social circle, all of whom have experienced their sons committing suicide. In every case no-one has the answer to why. All enjoyed solid, stable backgrounds.

A friend who is a BBC TV correspondent – his son committed suicide. A friend who is a film editor for Sky – his son committed suicide. And then there is Gary of course.

The bigger picture to all this is that there is something terribly, terribly wrong going on here. Why on earth are these people, who seemingly have everything going for them, making these terrible decisions? The figures are horrific for the number of suicides for men under the age of 45. I believe it's the second biggest killer.

In the aftermath of Gary's death, everyone was saying we've got to do more. But it's still clearly happening. There's something very wrong.

I think most people who lose someone in this manner put on a front but deep down they are never the same person again. The impact on those who are left is just monumental. You can never repair the damage.

There is no legislation for it. I do know that in nearly every conversation involving Gary I'm asked, why did he do it? The answer is always the same – I have absolutely no idea. People don't want to hear that. They almost demand a reason.

9

Parents' story

NEVER AT PEACE

*Roger and Carol Speed open up about their son's
remarkable life, tragic passing and legacy, and their
hope that others can learn from their experience*

Roger: When Gary came along, around two years after his sister Lesley, of course I dreamed that one day he might become a professional footballer.

Carol: I said: "What if he's not interested in football?!" Back came the reply: "Well, he's a boy isn't he? Of course he is going to be interested in football." Lesley herself has always enjoyed sport, always keeping fit. She's played tennis in the past. She doesn't have the same time now, too busy running a coffee shop in Reigate.

Roger: I soon had Gary playing football on the drive. He even managed to break one of the garage doors with the force of his shot. I would go in goal and have him shooting at me, using both feet. He was naturally left-footed but from a very young age I made sure he used his right foot as well.

Carol: I think we've got a photo of him kicking a ball at the age of 18 months. Another thing about Gary was from an early age he never liked to be late for anything. He was even born on the day he was due. Football-wise, Roger always felt Gary was going to be a decent player. I didn't really know either way.

I always felt he was going to make a better cricketer. He went on to play for Wales Under-11s at cricket. When he was 13 he just said: "That's it, I'm not playing cricket anymore." But at one stage he was playing football and cricket, plus table-tennis in the winter. He appeared to be a natural at sport.

Roger: Locally, he played for Aston Park Rangers, the ground just being down the road from where we lived. I was the manager.

Carol: The lads would get changed in a garage next to the hairdressers, the shop allowing them in there before and after games.

Roger: As the manager I had no trouble picking him to play because even from a young age he stood out. It's incredible how many players have been produced in the area. We've had Gary, Ian Rush, Michael Owen, Kevin Ratcliffe, Barry Horne. If you stretch it a bit there's also Mickey Thomas, Joey Jones and Robbie Savage. If they had all been the same age we would have had a cracking Wales team. Michael Owen was born across the border in Chester but lived in North Wales and played all his junior football there.

Carol: Gary enjoyed his schooling, especially as he got older. I think he would have loved to have gone to university but football took over. He loved history although surprisingly he failed his O-Level. The teacher had told me there was no way he was going to fail but he did. He was very good at geography. Football was his great love and he made quick progress, being selected for Deeside Schools Under-11s at the age of eight. One of the teachers at Queensferry Primary School, Ron Bishop, who sadly isn't with us any longer, really encouraged him. Ron was football-mad, which suited Gary. He ended up playing more than 100 games for Deeside [a record eventually eclipsed by Michael Owen]. I remember Gary, when he was at Leeds United, presenting Michael with a prize for what he had achieved with Deeside Schools.

Roger: At the weekend, Gary played for Aston Park Rangers on a Saturday while on a Sunday he turned out for a team called Pegasus, whose best players would often go for trials at Manchester City. By now I would be taking him everywhere to games, clocking up a fair bit of mileage.

Carol: We'd often travel down to South Wales for games when he was playing for Deeside. A group of us would go down in a convoy to places like Swansea. It was the games against Swansea schools where Gary became friends with Chris Coleman. Gary captained Deeside while Chris was captain of Swansea schools.

Roger: Playing for Pegasus, he was asked to go for trials at Manchester City but nothing came of it. It was a fair way for him to go because they played their games at Ashton – more travelling in the car! By that time Leeds United were interested in him.

Carol: He was spotted by a Leeds scout when he was playing a game in South Wales. He was asked to go for trials there.

Chester also wanted him and that's where I wanted him to go because it was local and he would be able to still live at home. But as far as Gary was concerned it was no contest. Leeds United was a far bigger club than Chester and with a great football history. Although he was spotted playing in Wales, ironically he was never selected for Wales Schools Under-15s, which was a surprise to everyone else who had seen him play.

Eddie Gray was the Leeds manager at the time and so Roger and I went up to see him. Gary was placed on the YTS scheme which was in operation at the time. I didn't really want him to go because obviously it meant him leaving home and he was only 16. He went into digs in an area of Leeds called Seacroft. It was awful. I cried all the way home thinking he was so far away from his family at a young age. It was too young really and he quickly became homesick. Nobody took any notice of me. It was all about wanting him to become a professional footballer.

Roger: I don't think what happened to him did him any harm in the long run. He had to grow up quickly.

Carol: He would write a lot because there were no mobile phones and he didn't like to use the phone in the digs. If Roger was on the right shift at work he would go up to see him play on the Saturday morning and then bring him back home. If Roger was working, Gary would have to get the bus from Leeds to Liverpool and we'd pick him up from Lime Street station, complete with all his washing which had to be sorted and ironed by Sunday teatime when he was taken to get the train back to Leeds. This was before he learned to drive. When he passed his test he bought himself an old Ford Escort.

But I didn't like him driving on the motorways, I would always be worried.

After Eddie Gray left, Billy Bremner took over as Leeds manager and we went up to see him. Billy didn't really know much about Gary but he took a look at him and decided to keep him on.

Billy Bremner came and went and was succeeded by Howard Wilkinson, who offered Gary a professional contract. But he also told Gary he wanted to speak to myself and Roger. That was a nice gesture. Howard wanted to make sure everything was right.

Roger: That was typical of Howard. He was a proper manager who tried to look after the players and treated them as people, not just footballers. It meant more trips for me to watch Gary and at work it meant juggling shifts. I could be working mornings, afternoons or nights. If I needed to go to a game I would try to get people to swap shifts. Usually it worked out okay.

Carol: We were very proud when it worked out for Gary at Leeds. It was Roger's dream come true. He had come a long way from smashing the garage and playing football with a pair of rolled-up socks on the stairs. He would kick anything. I used to play heck with him. I'd always be saying: "Can you not walk without kicking something?!" He couldn't even walk up the stairs without kicking something.

When he found himself in the Leeds first team we would go up to Elland Road for every home game. We'd try and go to all the away matches as well. My mother would come as well. She loved going to the games.

Roger: They soon ended up winning the league and I

managed to get on the bus which took the championship trophy around the city with all the players.

Carol: I missed out because I had gone away on holiday with my mum and sister. We'd booked this break in Spain not knowing of course that Leeds were going to win the league.

Roger: I can still remember having a few celebratory drinks with Gary and his big mate David Batty on the bus. They were great mates.

Carol: He was very friendly with other players as well. He followed Gordon Strachan and what he did very closely. When he was training, although he was a lot younger than Gordon, he wasn't able to match him in the routines they did. He started wondering why and quizzed Gordon, wanting to know what his secret was. He got into Gordon's fitness regime, the diet, exercises, everything. The healthy eating, yoga, pilates. Really, that was why he was able to play until he was 39.

Roger: Gordon was a big help to Gary in his career.

Carol: After Leeds he moved to Everton. I was made up because now he would be back living in the area. He rented first before buying a house in Rossett. It was lovely because he was virtually on the doorstep after all those years away in Leeds. Ed was born, which was fantastic, especially him being so close to his grandparents.

A few years later, Gary called me quite late one night to say he was off to Newcastle. It was a complete shock to me. My immediate reaction as his mother was to say: "You can't go up at this time of night!" He said no, he was going and he signed for Newcastle, where Kenny Dalglish was the manager. I think this was his happiest time as a player. He loved it there and never wanted to leave.

We would got to as many matches as we could, although it wasn't as easy as travelling up to Leeds.

Roger: The atmosphere at St. James' Park was terrific. But it was a long, long drive. You always knew, as soon as the game finished, you were confronted with the long trip home.

Carol: Sometimes we would stay over depending what shift Roger was on. Gary had a lovely house up there near Morpeth. He wasn't happy leaving Newcastle to go to Bolton. I don't think Bobby Robson, who was the manager, knew much about it. He was told Gary was being sold. Bobby had called Gary his blue-chip player, which had been some compliment. Gary thought a lot about Bobby as well. He later ran the London Marathon in support of Sir Bobby's charity.

After Bolton, where he enjoyed his time with Sam Allardyce, it was off to Sheffield United. But there he had problems with his back which necessitated surgery. He knew his playing career was slowing down now.

Roger: They were very good to him there, allowing him to go into coaching and then, of course, making him the manager.

Carol: He wasn't manager of Sheffield United for too long, with Wales wanting him to be their manager. I was quite surprised he took the Wales job. For me it appeared a bit too soon because he had only really started his managerial career. He told me: "You don't turn your country down."

Roger: Yes, he's always loved his country and was a proud Welshman. He's the only one in the family! The rest of us are English.

I'll never forget the year we were married – 1966 – England won the World Cup! Although of course with Gary, at times I've become an honorary Welshman. I suppose I support

Wales ahead of England now. It was fantastic going to see him in his office in Cardiff after he became Wales manager. It was a feeling I will never forget. It sent a tingle down my spine.

Carol: It was nice that Chris Coleman took over from Gary, although it must have been bittersweet for him. They had been big friends for years, so if anyone could step into Gary's shoes it was Chris. It was nice that he kept Gary in his thoughts whenever he was with Wales.

Roger: He dedicated some of the success Wales had in the European Championship in France in 2016 to Gary.

I was asked to say a few words to the Wales players before the friendly game against Costa Rica in Cardiff three months after Gary's passing, which was a memorial game for him. To be honest it wasn't as hard as I had first imagined to speak in the dressing room. I wrote out what I was going to say. I was made up after I had done it, to be honest. I had surprised myself.

Carol: Ed gave a marvellous speech in one of the rooms before the game in the Cardiff Stadium, absolutely amazing for a boy who was just 13. He had everyone in tears. I didn't even know he was going to speak. For a young lad to do what he did...

Roger: He was unbelievable. It took your breath away.

Carol: It proved to be wonderful celebration of Gary's life. I know he is our lad but since he has gone we have never heard a bad word said against him. We've got lovely memories but no answers. All the time your mind thinks about why.

Roger: We haven't got a clue.

Carol: If you don't know the reason it happened you are never at peace, really. If you're physically ill, people can see you are physically ill. We didn't know there was anything wrong with Gary. You never recover from anything like this. Never. It's the biggest shock anyone could ever experience.

Roger: At such an early age, deary me.

Carol: People on the outside looking in would think he had everything going for him. But something was troubling him.

Roger: There's been some brilliant people trying to help us. Chris Coleman, for instance, has been good whenever I've met him.

Carol: It doesn't get any easier. I think you can live with it more if, say, it was a car accident. Or if you knew he was ill, or could see he was ill, but we didn't know anything. One minute he was here and the next he was gone.

One thing it's done, I hope, is that it has helped open the doors for people to talk about any mental issues. All we can think is that Gary was suffering from depression, although you'd never have known. He would put a smile on his face all the time. But that's a man thing, isn't it?

Roger: I just hope people can learn from our experience.

Carol: I hardly watch football anymore.

Roger: No, Carol won't watch football.

Carol: It's too much for me if I watch it. I can still see him there playing. So I can't do it, no. I can't watch it.

Roger: I still watch football but maybe not as many matches as I used to. I'm patron of the local Welsh Premier League side Connah's Quay Nomads. I'll go and watch them.

Carol: There's a great legacy to Gary in the area. For instance, when they were about to build some new houses they asked the children from the local schools what they wanted to call some of the roads. They chose Llys Gary Speed [Gary Speed

Court]. Where he used to play for Aston Park Rangers has been turned into a children's playground, with a memorial written on slate to him.

Roger: When it was a football pitch we had a game after our daughter Lesley and Tony got married, between the northerners and the southerners. Gary was the referee but ended up scoring the winning goal for the northerners. He wasn't allowing our son-in-law's side to win!

Carol: It's lovely going there knowing it should always be there, along with the street that has been named after him. Some people have said to me "Oh, Gary wouldn't have liked that" because he was quiet and unassuming. He probably wouldn't go along with it if he was still here but now I don't think he will begrudge us doing it.

We started up golf events in his memory, along with a charity in his name. There was a wonderful response with lots of people from football lending their support. We did it for four years and there is still money to be distributed. After that we will wind it up. Yes, there have been some lovely memories because he was a good lad.

Roger: It's nice that the two boys, Ed and Tommy, take after him.

Carol: They have turned out lovely lads. What happened to them at such a young age... Roger has carried on taking them all over the place, something he did when Gary was alive because he was often away or too busy to take them to their sporting venues, so Roger would always step in.

They are both studying in America but I'm sure one day they will both be back. Luckily, Tommy has packed in his boxing. I only went to see him box once and I remember twisting these leather gloves I had been wearing because I was so worried about him getting hurt. I vowed never to go again.

After Gary died I used to take Tommy to Warrington for his practice sessions but I would just drop him off. I couldn't watch him.

Roger: He was very good young boxer but one day just decided to give it up.

Carol: A bit like Gary giving up on the cricket when he was a lad.

10

Friends' story

OPENING UP

Kevin Nolan

Became good pals with Gary when they played
alongside each other for Bolton

Hearing the awful news about Speedo still sends shivers down my spine. I was with West Ham training. It was a cool down day and we were sitting down having some food. The manager Sam Allardyce was on the next table and he received a phone call from Steve Bruce. You heard Sam go "You must be joking" and his face had gone white. It looked so dramatic that you knew something serious had gone on. He looked over to me and said I wasn't going to believe it but Speedo had killed himself.

I just went, "What?" After that it was like I was in a complete daze. "Speedo? No. Surely not?" Without a shadow of doubt you thought that Speedo was the last person who would have been capable of doing something as horrific as this.

I'd only spoken to him three or four days earlier. The usual chit chat, nothing out of the ordinary. We talked about getting together and sharing a beer with our wives. It doesn't get any easier thinking about it now. I still feel my body shaking. I still can't believe it and I certainly can't explain it.

He was such a beautiful man and that shone through in everything he did. He was somebody I looked up to and I was just thankful I got to know him on a personal as well as a professional level. He has helped my career no end, especially looking closely at his leadership qualities as a captain. And as a man off the field, how he conducted himself made a huge impression and has remained with me.

I first really got to know him when he signed for Bolton from Newcastle. He was 35 and everybody thought he was over the hill. Sam Allardyce, though, had that knack of bringing in players who everyone thought were finished. But it was still a big fee for someone of his age, something like £750,000. It just showed what Sam knew about Speedo and what he could still produce because once he arrived you knew he was still class. The way he was off the pitch, always wanting to help you.

You could see how fit he was. He was at the front of everything in training. He would always push himself. He also had that smile which was infectious. It made you want to train harder.

I can still picture him standing next to Sam in the training ground on his first day. I was a young lad then and I just went up to him to wish him all the best. We'd had a few moments as opponents in past games and he had a laugh and a joke about that. We just got on with it and ended up as great mates.

That, though, didn't stop me from looking up to him as an idol and a hero. With that in mind I would always want to pick his brains on anything. He was so open and helpful. He was brilliant for me.

He also had a great knowledge about other sports. He loved his boxing, cricket and golf. He even got me into cricket. I couldn't stand cricket. There was nothing about it that I liked. I wouldn't play it at school.

Within a short time, through Speedo, I was sitting there in front of the telly, before we went into the gym, watching cricket with him explaining all the rules. Now I'm really into it and watch it all the time. I was soon being absorbed by the 2005 Ashes watching Freddie Flintoff and everyone against the Aussies. He told me about his experience facing the fast bowler Simon Jones. He said Simon just launched one at him and he didn't even see the ball until it was too late. Getting into cricket was just an amazing thing for me and that was down to just one person, Speedo.

I know Speedo also loved his boxing. I think he was quite a tasty boxer himself. He loved it when we got the boxing pads out in pre-season. He would go around giving everyone a kidney jab, things like that. Maybe he chose football to save his good looks. But to be fair, for someone who was so good-looking he still put himself in some physical situations on the football field. You thought, 'Careful, you are going to get your head kicked off there,' but he was up for it. He was always determined and wanted to be a winner. He had the heart of a lion. He never liked losing. The number of times the two of us would argue in training when we were on opposite sides because we both wanted to win. We used to smash into one another. His competitive instinct certainly brought the best out of me.

One of the biggest compliments I can give him was when he was out injured, Jay-Jay Okocha was the club captain and Speedo the vice-captain. He missed a few matches and with Jay-Jay also not playing the gaffer gave me the captain's armband. We ended up winning all the games. Against Charlton, Speedo was fit again and back in the side. Without saying anything to Speedo, Sam told the kitman to place the captain's armband on my peg. Anyone else in that dressing room would have lost their head if that had happened to them but Speedo just came over to me and said I deserved it and shook my hand.

There was no jealousy. There was no tossing off the afternoon. He was a true professional, the class just oozed out of him. I ended up scoring because he made me feel like 100 men. We won 1-0. I put my display that day down to him because his actions had made me feel so special. I knew he was backing me. He was right behind me.

They were little things but important to me. If he was still here today he probably wouldn't remember things like this. He was a top-class bloke with a beautiful family. The two lads doted on him and I would often see his parents, Roger and Carol, and Louise, Gary's wife.

Our friendship became stronger and stronger. We enjoyed our nights out and Hayley, my wife, got on well with Louise.

Ironically, I later moved to Newcastle where he had played and still had friends there. It helped produce a nice circle of friends. I remember we were out for a Christmas do and for around six weeks before, Speedo – being the ultimate professional – hadn't had a drink. This night, though, he helped make up for that with a good few drinks.

Unfortunately, because of this he couldn't make it out of a taxi before being sick. You can imagine the taxi driver wasn't too happy. So after helping out Speedo to bed, I then had to go back and clean the taxi. The next morning I don't think I've seen him so quiet and sheepish. He just went: "Thanks Nobby lad."

At training I used to smile to myself because it was almost a tradition. He would tell everyone: "I'm too old for this shit and you're getting f**k all out of me today." Then he ends up being the best player, running around like a lunatic as if he was 17 again. I have to confess I carried on those sayings when I got to Newcastle and continued them on until the end of my playing career.

He would always try and help. When I was about to go to Newcastle he rang me and said he was fearful of me going there because he knew there was a lot going on behind the scenes. I appreciated the advice but told him I needed to get away from Bolton because I had been going through a really bad patch. He understood that but didn't want me going into the unknown. That was the class of the man.

Seeing what Speedo was about helped me. I knew I had to prove to the Newcastle fans that I wanted to be there. You have got to show them you care. He was the one who drilled that into me. Prove that and they will give everything back. He gave me the platform. I knew what the Newcastle supporters expected.

I knew he loved his days at Newcastle because when he was at Bolton he would be singing all the Newcastle songs.

Pride of place in my son's games room is a big portrait of myself and Speedo hugging after a game. It's a really lovely photo which my mum and dad bought for me after Speedo died. The photo means so much to me because of the huge influence he had on my career.

Why he ended it all I'll never understand. I remember one day talking about Speedo with Joey O'Brien, who was with me at Bolton and West Ham. He was another one who had looked up to Speedo. We sat there and went through everything. When it happens to someone else you immediately think, 'Oh, someone must have realised something wasn't right.'

But with Speedo I don't think anyone – even the family – realised what was going on in Speedo's head. I questioned myself. Did he look any different the day before he died when he appeared on Football Focus. No, he looked fine. Professionally, he was transforming Wales into a team that was becoming competitive. Chris Coleman probably ended up reaping the rewards of that.

There's nothing I can put my finger on as a clue to what happened. That's the most frustrating and gutting thing because you want to find a reason. Everyone loved Speedo, so no matter what he was going through we would have all been there to support him. If there was a problem I just wished he could have picked up the phone and I would have been there wherever I was. There's probably another 1,000 people who would have done that as well. That's the saddest thing.

I wish he could have seen how many people loved and adored

him. He was very emotional and compassionate but there was probably inside him something he couldn't show.

Osian Roberts

Football Association of Wales technical director who was Gary's right-hand man with the national team

I was out in Qatar putting on a coaching symposium. It was a three-day course and I had spoken to Gary before I flew out to Doha. He was really excited about the arrangements we had made for the summer, including a game against Mexico in New York. He was really made up that we had finalised that friendly. Right from the beginning for him it was all about the players wanting to turn up for Wales games.

Down the years, that hadn't always been the case. We had in the past – and quite rightly so – been criticised by Wales fans who saw players fail to turn up for international games claiming they were injured but then turning out for their club sides the next weekend. Also, a number of players had retired from playing for their country at a fairly young age.

As manager he wanted to bring back the feel-good factor among the players. Players wanting to turn up and enjoying being part of the Wales squad. All this had to come from within them. There was no way you can force them to join in. That was happening under Gary and the trip to New York at the end of the season was, in some respects, a reward for them. They would have a week in New York around playing a prestige friendly, being able to enjoy some downtime, relax and go and see the city.

We had also been talking about me while I was in Doha, looking to see if I could sort out some warm weather training in the future for the squad. Everything was about planning for the future. He was looking forward to what we had in mind.

So when the news broke about his death I was just left stunned, astounded – unable, like most people, to comprehend what had occurred.

While I was conducting the coaching symposium I had left my mobile phone in the hotel room. When I returned I had all these missed calls and messages off my wife. It was like: "Have you heard the news about Gary?" The rumours were breaking through. I rang her and she confirmed the news he was dead. I couldn't believe it. I was still hoping that because the news was still breaking that it was just one wild rumour.

Then, when it was obviously true, you just assume he had been involved in a car crash, something like that.

I felt completely alone out there in Qatar, with no real access to the news and all this going around in my head. I thought at first I should go home immediately. But then after thinking it through I thought to myself, 'I get home and then what? What use would I be?' The family will obviously be grieving but really it wasn't the right time for me to visit them. After speaking to my wife I decided to stay, which was a good thing in some ways as for a few hours at least I was able to take my mind off the tragic event. With no real news outlet in Qatar, I also missed a lot of the talk about Gary's death. Whether that was a good thing or not I don't know.

As men sometimes we are not great at opening up and, for

me, maybe the coaching sessions were an escape. Gary, as it has now proved, was a great example of someone who couldn't open up. I was able to bottle my raw emotions in the work out there. What he had done didn't make any sense whatsoever. I still can't understand it today if I'm honest.

The fact there hasn't been any answers has probably given more column inches over the years to the circumstances of his death. It has given some people the opportunity to make some remarks and speculate and, of course, Gary isn't here to answer them. I just know what happened didn't add up to the person I had known well. You go through the process of racking your brain for any clues about why he might have taken the action he did. Were there any signs? For me there was nothing surrounding Gary which was out of the ordinary. He might have been frustrated and disappointed at times with certain things – as we all are – but nothing where you imagine Gary was thinking, 'Bloody hell, I've got to take that drastic action.'

I went to the funeral and then it was a case of trying to sort things out with Wales. The funeral was just the most horrific experience, really. I was so glad to be there but at the same time it was unbearable. I couldn't face the wake afterwards. It was too much. In the church I sat in between Gary McAllister and Simon Grayson. The tears flowed constantly. It was so sad.

Alan Shearer spoke incredibly well. It's sometimes said there are no real friends in football. Gary was certainly the exception to that feeling. He was a true friend to many in the game, something Alan portrayed so well in his eulogy. Then one of Gary's boys, Ed, spoke, which was just incredible. He was amazingly brave but was determined to say a few words about his dad. Tom was also so brave on the day. I think the fact Ed spoke made it even more difficult emotionally.

Then we had the friendly against Costa Rica, which was to be a memorial game at the end of February for Gary, to sort out. It was the family's wishes that myself and Raymond Verheijen [Wales' assistant manager] were in charge for the match. For whatever reason he didn't respect their wishes and so I was left on my own, really. Chris Coleman had been appointed as Gary's successor but didn't feel it right that he should be involved in this game. Since we lost he's quite happy to say it was my match!

That week, the Wales camp was all about the players and the staff. It had been the first time since Gary's death that everybody had met up. I got them together with the analysis team who had created this montage of Gary as a player and coach. I knew his passing wasn't something we could brush under the carpet. This was more about being concerned with the mental health of the players.

I felt it was important to have an opportunity to talk about him and what had happened. We needed to get together. We needed to hug each other. We needed to help one another. There were a number of the players finding it very difficult to come to terms with his passing. As you can imagine, during the incredible montage there were plenty of tears. There were very few words uttered. It was all about everyone understanding that we were all there for one another. It was also important to talk and express any emotional concerns.

We had a psychiatrist in the hotel for anyone who wanted this support. A large contingent of the squad did take advantage of that assistance.

Bryn Law, who knew Gary well and reported on our games for Sky Sports, was there and revealed he had booked a room to film any of the players who wanted to talk about Gary but only if they felt up for it. There was no pressure to do any interviews.

Normally, when you're in charge of a game, the priority is the result. You want to play well, you want to perform, you want to entertain, but if you keep losing matches you're not going to last long in your job. For once that went out of the window. This was a psychological exercise and making certain Gary's family wishes were respected on the evening. We didn't want them going home feeling an opportunity had been missed, we wanted to ensure they got everything they wanted or needed that evening.

When Roger and the boys came down before the game and asked if they could come into the dressing room and speak to the players, there was only one answer – yes. Normally you are focussed on the match. This was the complete opposite, this was about respecting their wishes, so of course we welcomed them into the dressing room. Ed spoke to the players before they went out onto the pitch. You've got experienced players in the team who've heard most things during their careers. But this was special and they just sat there in admiration, looking at this young boy who had gone through so much and yet showing this maturity, level-headedness, call it what you will. Displaying incredible inner strength. The players couldn't believe it. For me, it was hard to watch. It was hard to keep your emotions in check.

I remember Ashley Williams, a real leader and strong character, someone who is a machine as a player, someone who never misses a game. Plays with injuries, a real warrior. At half-time he came into the dressing room and told me he couldn't move. His legs couldn't move. He's never felt like this before on a football pitch. The emotional stress, the mental stress of Gary's passing, had got to him. Who am I on the touchline to shout at him? You just had to respect what some of the players like Ash were going through.

For many it was about going through the process, getting through the evening. We wanted to win the game in memory of Gary but, realistically, we were in a completely different place and we ended up losing 1-0. But again it was about the family. No-one could have imagined what they were going through.

The nice thing was that Roger was involved with us in the 2016 European Championship when we managed to reach the semi-finals. I hope the family know – I'm sure they do – that the groundwork, the foundations of that success were laid by Gary. Chris Coleman built the walls on it.

Gary had changed the environment of Wales international football, changed the culture, which meant making some difficult decisions. He put some hard rules in place initially. He had to confront some senior players about certain things but he wasn't afraid to do that. He made certain we got what we needed to try and improve the squad and everything around it.

He wanted all the players to sing the national anthem. Some of them would have to learn the words, not the easiest assignment for a new manager. He had a brainwave. Instead of us doing it amongst ourselves he got the Miss Wales, Courtenay Hamilton, a classically trained singer, who used to sing the national anthem in those days, to come along and teach the players. All of a sudden they just bought into it!

Another early decision was to make Aaron Ramsey captain, the youngest in Wales' history. We had a shortlist of possibilities but in the end went with Aaron. Gary had faith in him and felt he would mature into the role. Maybe he saw a bit of himself in Aaron because Gary possessed leadership qualities from a young age.

He later lost the captaincy after Chris took over but Aaron still led, especially in the big games. We missed him badly in the Euro 2016 semi-final against Portugal after he was suspended. He was a key component in big matches.

Gary had taken over halfway thorough a European Championship qualifying group knowing we couldn't qualify for the 2012 finals. So we knew we had time to implement a plan. We wanted to break it down into sections, with everything aimed at qualifying for the 2014 World Cup finals in Brazil. It was all in the players' minds from Gary becoming manager of Wales that it was all about Brazil. With that the goal, we would always have the Brazil logo on things to keep it at the forefront of everyone' minds. It wasn't about now, it was about putting things in place for Brazil.

With Gary it wasn't all serious stuff. There were plenty of laughs and humour. We might show alongside the technical stuff a nice slide of a beautiful Brazilian girl on the Copacabana beach in Rio de Janeiro – this was our goal to be part of all this. It helped make it at times light-hearted but the message was there, we wanted to be part of Brazil 2014. We wanted everyone to enjoy the journey.

Shortly after taking over, he presented the Wales Under-16s with their international caps. Managing them was part of my coaching responsibilities. He said openly that he wanted to implement at first-team level what I had introduced at Under-16s level, so that proved early on that we had the same vision, the same ideas about how to play, the same philosophy.

He used to come down to Cardiff on a day off when he was at Sheffield United and do a couple of coaching sessions with the Under-16s, talk to the players and staff and drive back up to Yorkshire. That was in his own free time. He would help inspire the younger generation by his presence. So when he arrived as Wales manager he was already aware of what we were doing at that level and wanted to replicate it with the senior team.

We became tight on what was becoming the Wales identity, our way of playing. It was to be done over six phases. Sadly, when he passed away we had only completed three. At first, implementing our ideals, we knew we might have to take some hits. But as a young manager he was so brave. We knew, slowly behind the scenes, things were falling into shape.

There were even moments when some sections of the media were questioning his position as Wales manager. Some people couldn't see the progress being made behind the scenes. He had a clear plan. And when we lost him I saw it as my responsibility to see this through, that we didn't stop after three phases.

We were fortunate that Chris took over. He could have brought in his own staff and done it his way. He would have been well within his rights to have done that. I sat down with him. I didn't know him, I'd never even met him. I told him that I got it, he would want to bring in his own staff and work his way. I was still Wales' technical director and I would help him with any knowledge or information of the work we had done with Gary as manager.

He replied that he was a big believer in learning new things – that he had gone to manage in Europe with the intention of becoming a better coach. He added that what Speedo had put in place was what he believed in. And if I was good enough for Speedo than I was good enough for him.

So off we went and it was really enjoyable.

Chris Coleman

Led Wales to the 2016 European Championship finals
after taking over as manager from his childhood friend

I was out in Cyprus managing AEL Limassol and was in my office an hour before we were due to play a game. My phone was going off all the time, which I felt was strange because anybody who knows me would never try to contact me on the morning of a match. They know that I would never get back to them so they would be wasting their time.

But I noticed Lee Clark, who was a big friend, had sent me a message so I read it and couldn't believe what I was reading. He was telling me that Gary was dead and that he had hanged himself. My first reaction was – no chance. That can't be true. This is all a great mistake, it was the wrong information.

We went ahead and played the game but I can't remember too much of it because I was mostly sat in the dugout in a complete daze. The actual match was passing me by. All I'm thinking about was Gary and what was supposed to have happened. Nobody else around me would have known him so I felt very much alone with my thoughts.

In the press conference after the game, someone asked me about Gary. By then the news had broken back in the UK and the awful event had been confirmed. I was just numb. It had now really hit home. I'd also spoken to my dad on the phone. We had both known Speedo since he and I were 10. I was playing for Swansea schools and he represented Deeside. Really, from those days we had become great friends.

My dad had confirmed the news to me. Even now, talking about him, I get goosebumps. That horrible, horrible day will never go away.

The problems I was having at the time with the AEL president paled into insignificance at losing one of my biggest mates in football. In the end I walked out in the January because no-one was getting paid.

I called up Gary's dad Roger – a phone call I wasn't looking forward to making. I'd got to know the family, especially Roger, very well. I just couldn't imagine what he and Carol were going through. It was a very, very tough time.

Roger and my dad were very similar in that they would take their sons everywhere. We used to talk about them in glowing terms whenever we met up as players in the Wales squad. We appreciated what they had both done for us. They both loved their football and whenever they were in our company we'd have a laugh and share a joke. They supported us as kids, nothing was too much for them if they knew it was helping us improve as footballers.

They would take us to our games. Give us what we needed. So obviously I'd known the Speed family for many years. In the end it was more than football which brought us so close. We shared so many interests outside football.

The first time I saw him, it was a two-legged Welsh Schools Under-11s final, Swansea against Deeside, with the first leg at Swansea.

I think we lost 3-0 or 3-1. We lost the second leg in North Wales 2-1 and he was the standout player. Technically, he was way above everybody else.

You looked at him and thought, 'Christ, who's this kid here?' I remember saying to my dad that the No10 [Speedo] was a hell of a good player. My father agreed, adding that he felt he was "a proper player".

We didn't strike up any real conversation. I just remember shaking his hand and thinking this is the best player in Wales at this age. I had instant respect for him, even though I didn't really know anything about him.

The next time I saw him was in an Under-13s final when Swansea played Flintshire. This time we were too strong for them and ended up beating them. It was a one-off game this time around and we played at the Vetch Field, which was then Swansea's ground.

I went to Manchester City when I was 14 for a trial and there he was – Speedo was having a trial with the club as well. We got talking and just hit it off.

That bond continued when we both travelled to Aberystwyth

for trials for the Wales Under-15s side. We enjoyed a great relationship from then on until the day he left us.

Incredibly, Speedo was never capped at Wales Under-15s level. It's unbelievable to this day, almost laughable, especially as I played five or six times for the team. I remember saying to him: "How the hell can't you get into this team?"

Thankfully, it didn't hold him back and he ended up signing for Leeds United when he left school, while I was taken on by Manchester City. But we ended up together again playing for Wales Under-18s followed by the Under-21s. I can honestly never ever remember him having a bad game. He was such a talented, complete player.

We roomed together, we were very young, a couple of rum buggers who enjoyed the good times as well as being dedicated to becoming good professional footballers. I suppose we were looked upon as being a pair of good-lookers but I think I was a level below him, mind you! I remember we were both playing for the Under-21s one day and my family came to watch. I've got two older sisters. My eldest sister was completely besotted. After that he used to take the mickey out of me because he knew she fancied him. He could be my future brother-in-law!

When we advanced into the senior Wales set-up we often roomed together. It would be either Gary, Dean Saunders or Ryan Giggs. We would chop and change a bit. Even if we weren't rooming together, we would be together. We couldn't wait to meet up for Wales games.

Neither of us could understand when some other Wales players didn't turn up for matches, coming up with all sorts of excuses. Speedo and I couldn't wait to turn up. We'd be looking at the calendar thinking, 'There's only three more weeks to the next Wales game.' The days couldn't go by quick enough. We just absolutely loved it, the camaraderie, the togetherness. The pride of representing Wales. It was everything for us. There was such a great team spirit. We'd have an absolute ball.

The saddest thing was missing out as players on the big stage – a World Cup or European Championship finals. The biggest kick in the teeth was in 1993 when we just failed to reach the World Cup finals in the USA, losing to Romania in Cardiff. I felt absolutely sick in the dressing room after the game and then travelling along the M4 back to London, where I was playing for Crystal Palace, was horrendous. I felt completely empty and destroyed.

Even on the Saturday I was still feeling the effects of the Wales game. We were playing Barnsley away and my head was elsewhere. Alan Smith was the manager at the time and he pulled me and said: "For f***'s sake, shake yourself up." I replied: "I can't boss. My head is in pieces." We had come so close and at the 11th hour the chance to play in USA '94 had passed us by. It had been a right kick in the bollocks. I can still see Paul Bodin's penalty smashing against the bar.

Reaching the finals would have been great for the Wales manager Terry Yorath. He'd had a really bad time. He had lost his boy Daniel while they were both playing football in the garden. Danny was only 15 but died of a heart problem. He was a really good young player at that age, too. There were big hopes for him as a future professional player. Terry showed such courage and strength of character to carry on and almost take us to the finals of the World Cup. We had a good team and he deserved to go to a tournament. In the end it was sheer bad luck which denied him. I felt sorry for Terry more than anything.

Then, of course, both Gary and I ended up as managers of Wales, which was an amazing coincidence considering how we had both started off, meeting each other as 10-year-olds.

We both went for the job after John Toshack left. We ended up both being interviewed. He was the manager of Sheffield United and he called me to say that he could soon be out of the door at Sheffield United because the results hadn't been great. I told him to just grin and bear it, to keep his head down. It was his first job and he was still learning. I told him I was in for the Wales job and he said I'd end up getting it.

Later, the Football Association of Wales contacted Sheffield United to ask whether they could also interview Speedo. To be fair, he contacted me and revealed that they also wanted to speak to him. We were both laughing and joking knowing we were now rivals for the Wales job. We'd come a long way since our schools matches.

He ended up getting it and around a week later he rang me up. He said: "Cookie, where are you?" I said I'd just dropped the kids off at school and I was just kicking about. He said that I'd love this big leather chair he was sitting in! He was in the Wales office in Cardiff. He was enjoying taking the piss out of me.

We were able to laugh and joke. Nothing could break the friendship. Then, of course, I did become Wales manager but in horrible circumstances. It was the hardest decision I've ever had to make – but someone had to take over after he died.

I took it on but quickly discovered it was going to be a lot harder than I had ever imagined. The whole team, the staff, everyone was still in mourning. But there was still a job to be done because Speedo had sparked a recovery and there were high hopes for the squad.

The trouble was, under me, we were now losing games. My head was all over the place. It became obvious we weren't ready to move on from losing Gary. We were stuck in what had happened – we weren't able to move on. It was really tough, probably the toughest time I've ever had.

At times I thought to myself, 'Jesus Christ, what have I done?' On an emotional level I was battling against the tide. Normally, when you go into a job you know what you're going to be dealing with. This was in many ways a trip into the unknown. I was fighting many battles and clearly losing them all. It was all too raw, too new. None of us were ready to move on. Really, you never learn to move on, you just learn to deal with the situation better. Initially it was bloody tough.

I'd taken over on March 1, St. David's Day. I remember getting all the players in a room to have a chat. I said a few words about Gary. I knew he's had a big impact on some of them, like Aaron Ramsey. I know they had thought a lot about him and many were still in shock. They didn't know how to deal with his passing.

Dressing rooms can be brutal places at times, with people quickly coming in with their banter. There was none of that. It was a weird atmosphere. It was very cold with few shafts of light. If you compared the atmosphere then to the one we experienced in reaching the European Championship semi-finals in 2016, you wouldn't have believed the turnaround. It's the biggest difference I've ever seen in a group of the same players.

At first I don't think we were bothered about trying to win football matches. Nothing seemed right because he wasn't there. I ended up with the supporters giving me stick and it probably boiled down to the fact I wasn't Gary Speed. They wanted him. It wouldn't have mattered who had come in. It wouldn't work at first because he wouldn't be Gary Speed. Everyone loved him. That was the huge impact he had made in a short time.

I know he would have been proud of what I eventually achieved with the squad. I was always proud of him – he was my mate. When he was managing Wales I still felt part of it because we were very close. If he laughed, I laughed. If he suffered, I suffered.

It was nice that Roger Speed was part of our adventure in the European Championship. It was an open door for Roger. He had been down to the training ground and at one stage, shortly after I had taken over, he came into the dressing room and said a few words to the players. He told them they had to get their heads around what had happened and to do their best for me. He added that Gary would be beside me, urging the team on. It was great and meant a lot to me what he said. In defying the odds and reaching the semi-finals, I always felt Gary was at my side sharing in some great days.

Everyone questions why Gary decided to do what he did. I can honestly say as a close mate I never envisaged him ever being able to contemplate anything like this. You always think, have we missed something? He was the last person – I can't emphasise that enough – the last person who would have done this. No way would you link the events of that tragic night with him.

I still think about it. I honestly can't get my head around it. I lost my dad around five years ago. He was 70-odd and I'm a grown man, and I was in absolute pieces, crushed. So I can't imagine what the two boys, Ed and Tommy, went through at such a young age. Just crushing.

Dan Walker

*Interviewed Gary on Football Focus
the day before his death*

I was in church and my phone, which was on silent, kept buzzing with text after text and phone call after phone call. I was sat with my wife and children and told them something pretty important must have happened, so I would have to pop outside to check the phone for a few moments.

Before I was able to check any of the messages or see who had rung me, I received another call and this time it was Alan Shearer. I know Alan quite well but I still found it weird that he had rung me on a Sunday morning.

He asked me if I had heard about Gary. Just the day before, Speedo had been on Football Focus, which I present, with Gary McAllister. I wasn't thinking clearly and I just answered: "Gary who?" He then went: "Speedo." The thing that shocked me was that Alan would always call him Speedo and never Gary. This time he had at first called him Gary. He then delivered the sickening news that Speedo was dead.

He explained more to me, but it was hard to take in

stood outside my local church in Sheffield. There were now other calls coming in, making it a strange and very sad morning.

It was almost impossible to accept because he had been on Football Focus the previous day and appeared just the same as normal, friendly and kind. He was someone who always asked questions about you and the family.

Gary McAllister and I have spoken since about that day when they had appeared on the programme, and we both agreed he had seemed so happy. What came across to both of us was how dedicated he was to the job of managing Wales. He had memorised all the fixtures for the forthcoming World Cup qualifying campaign. He could talk in great detail about all the opponents.

He seemed so committed on a professional level which again, apart from his personal responsibilities, made it so hard to comprehend what he ended up doing. I don't think I've ever got my head around it to this day.

Putting Speedo on with Gary McAllister was a natural fit because they had been mates for years, both playing for Leeds United of course.

As normal, Speedo turned up and said hello to everyone. One of the cameramen went up to him and told him he had gone to the same school as Gary. They ended up chatting for five minutes talking about their days at the school.

Speedo then came over to me and asked me how my kids were, the normal friendly conversation. He was someone who was always genuinely interested in other people.

I had seen him a couple of months earlier and he had looked a bit tired. But on this occasion he looked really healthy and full of the joys of life. He talked about his own family and was excited about the professional challenge which lay ahead with Wales.

After the programme ended, I asked him if he wanted to go upstairs to see his big mate Alan Shearer, who was in the Match Of The Day office preparing for the programme that night. The three of us then sat for an hour or so watching the first half of the Premier League games that were on. It was just the normal football chat.

Afterwards, Alan said they should meet up the next week. I think the arrangement was for Speedo and his wife Louise to travel up to Alan's house the next Friday.

Speedo and I had tried to arrange a game of golf a few weeks back but one of us had to cancel. As he was leaving to go home he said: "Dan, give me a call on Monday and we will finally have this game of golf."

So when I received the tragic news your brain goes into overdrive. Just the day before, here was a guy clearly thinking about the future, eulogising about his kids, asking me to ring him on the Monday and planning to go round to the Shearers' place on the Friday. You then hear on the Sunday morning that for whatever reason he's gone. It took a long while to get all that through your head.

People have all got their theories about why. It's something I am still asked quite regularly because, of course, many people had seen Football Focus on that Saturday or would have later known all about it. They will ask me for my thoughts about what happened and why did it happen. I tell them I don't know. "But you were with him the day before, you must know something," they reply.

I didn't and since then Gary Mac and I have been over it, trying to analyse the day.

But for whatever reason, he and I didn't speak following that programme for around three weeks. We'd sent each other the odd text message but then Gary rang me and said, "Dan, I need to talk." We then spoke on the phone for ages talking about what had happened. What our thoughts were and trying to work out how Speedo had been that day.

I know it hit Gary hard and I think it's still tough for him now because they were big mates and because they were on the show together the day before Speedo's death. The three of us had been in the same room with him for about four hours.

I think all of us who knew Speedo quite well have spent hours wondering, could we have done anything? Were there any warning signs? You feel confused, then you feel guilty and then it's anger about why did he leave everyone? It's a strange mixture of emotions.

But one thing I do know is that there is still a lot of love and affection for him to this day. There remains a huge interest in his life.

I will never forget the huge outpourings of emotion at the Wales game against Costa Rica, which was dedicated to his memory. I was sat in a room with all his family and close friends. Everyone was struggling to come to terms with his passing.

In the years since, not just because of Speedo's story, I believe we have to be more open with one another and let people know if we are struggling mentally. Unless someone tells you, you usually have no idea of what they are going through, the private turmoil which might be going on in in their lives. Too many people can hide all that too well. It's also a reminder of the brevity of life – how it can suddenly be cut short.

Football isn't generally too open. You imagine many players act as if they don't have a single problem. It's improving to an extent but it's still not the environment where people open up. It's always been a macho industry.

I have spoken at length with people like Speedo's dad Roger and no-one can put their finger on why. It must be so hard on his family because of the huge question mark over Speedo's death. Ultimately, we still all miss him.

Matt Hockin

*Became very close to Gary during his role as
player liaison officer at Bolton*

Thinking about Speedo not being here still hurts me a lot. Sometimes, when you go to football grounds, you see ghosts. You go to White Hart Lane and you could still see the old team of the Sixties which was so successful. Now I look around our changing room at Burnley and see the lads laughing and think back to the happy days we had with Speedo when I was with him at Bolton.

I will never forget the days leading up to his death. By then I had moved to Blackburn as their player liaison officer and Gary was Wales manager. At Blackburn we had a young promising player called Adam Henley, who was eligible to represent Wales and the USA. The Thursday before his death, I had tried to get

Speedo on the phone to notify him about Adam. He rang back and the manager, Steve Kean, just happened to be stood opposite me. Speedo came on and his opening words were: "Oh Shocksy lad [Shocksy was his nickname for me because he said he never knew what I was going to do next]. Are you offering me the Blackburn job? What a mess at your club!" I just answered back: "Thanks for that Speedo, Keano is with me now!"

To be fair, he then asked to have a quick chat with Steve, whose job was under threat at the time. After Steve handed the phone back to me, we carried on our conversation, which had now turned from a bit of fun to being serious.

"Shocksy, I'm bored," he told me. "I'm really, really bored." I answered that there were plenty of things he could do with his spare time. He knew I would be in Cardiff on the Monday because the next night we were playing Cardiff in a cup game. I had decided in any case to travel down separately from the team, hoping to catch up with Speedo. He told me to come into the Football Association of Wales offices when I arrived and that I would be able to stay with him in the flat he occupied in Cardiff when he was on Wales business. Or he might book himself into the Blackburn team hotel. But we were definitely on for a meal and a few drinks. He was looking forward to a good old catch-up.

I was looking forward to it. I remember him clearly saying: "You can help me." I replied: "Okay. That's what I'm here for, anytime."

At Saturday lunchtime we were playing Stoke at their place – the day he appeared on Football Focus. That weekend I just didn't feel right. I had been going through some personal problems. That night, I stayed with Blackburn's club captain Ryan Nelson, who was injured. We went to a pub in Bowdon, Cheshire, where he lived. Had a few drinks and a nice meal.

The next day, the players were due in for training but I walked up to my car to travel to our training ground with a feeling which I can only describe as eerie. The morning felt so weird.

It was a similar experience to the one I had as a kid going to a Radio One Roadshow – only to learn when I got home that my nan had just suffered a stroke that day. This day in Bowdon, I just knew something wasn't right. As I drove it was strange. There appeared to be hardly anyone on the road. It was so surreal.

After getting to the training ground, I received a text message from Stephen Warnock, a player I knew from his Blackburn days. He was now with Aston Villa and was going down to Swansea on the team bus. His text broke the news of what had happened to Gary.

I walked into the swimming pool area at the training ground, saw the physio Dave Fevre, and just mumbled: "Speedo's dead." He told me to not be so stupid. But I told him that sadly it was true. He had killed himself. The rest of the day was horrible. I was gone.

Steve Kean told me I didn't have to travel with them to Cardiff. I did. I had to carry on. I was invited to the funeral. It was a really hard time. I can't help welling up now thinking about it all. It was so poignant, Blackburn playing in Cardiff.

Since our phone conversation, I had come up with a few ideas for him. I said being Wales manager opens up a few doors and maybe he should go and visits clubs like Juventus and Bayern Munich, and study their methods. To throw himself into various projects. I don't think the Wales job was enough for him – he had the energy to commit himself to other things in addition to that job. To be perfectly honest, I don't think anything was enough for him after he finished as a player. His whole life, I felt, was defined as Gary Speed the footballer.

I got that. I remember going to his holiday place in Saint-Tropez. We were with Bolton and it was an international break. Speedo had retired as a Wales player. He asked the manager Sam Allardyce if I could be given a few days off to join him for a short break in the south of France. Big Sam said yes, that was fine.

We flew over on the Monday morning and returned on the Wednesday night, and I think we spent the whole trip with him telling me how quickly he could sell his house and who was going to buy it. The whole thing had obviously taken over his head. So much so that at one stage I asked him, when was he going to relax? There seemed to be so much occupying his mind. He opened up about worrying about finishing playing and how the money wouldn't last for ever. All this, all that. I'm telling him he will okay. He had a great family behind him, everything would be fine.

I was at his last game as a player. By then he had moved on to Sheffield United, who were playing Wolves on a wet November day. He came off after around an hour. I was between clubs at the time and I just wanted to help him whenever I could. I'd done a lot with him over 12 months at Sheffield United. I took him into hospital when he underwent an operation on his back and I waited for him to wake up after the surgery. The next day, I drove him home to Chester to be with his wife

Louise. I was just in the background, supporting, helping. I genuinely loved the guy. He was a good, close mate.

One day, he had to travel to Leeds to have an injection in his back, but any idea of a quick return was out of the question because of a serious road traffic accident. He said we might as well go for a bit of lunch back in Leeds after he'd had the injection. I agreed and, over lunch, he was telling me some things about his past. How Howard Wilkinson had lectured him about going out too much as a young player, stories I was loving. Then he asked me whether I had read Sir Bobby Robson's autobiography. I told him I was meeting my mum in the Lake District the next week and I wanted to buy the book for her because she loved Sir Bobby. He said that we should go to Waterstones in Leeds to buy it and he could flick through it on the way back to see what he had said about Speedo.

We couldn't believe it. We get to Waterstones and there is a big notice informing everyone that Bobby is due there that day to sign copies of his book. He didn't want to go into the store. "I can't go in. I can't see him," he argued. I couldn't believe it. He always loved being Gary Speed the footballer but would never use that to gain an advantage for Gary Speed the person.

I remember helping move into his house and he asked me to call a sound system installation company for him. I did and said it was for Gary Speed the footballer. In a nice manner he warned me never to do that again. He didn't want any favours.

So I decided to go alone to purchase the book and get it signed by Bobby, and then went away to buy a different book. Speedo came up to me and asked what Bobby had said and was he now by himself? I said yes, he's on his own. So he finally went to see him. The looks on both of their faces when they saw each other was heart-warming. "Alright gaffer," said Speedo. "I didn't think you would remember me." Bobby replied: "I always remember the good players, Speedo." All the way back he was buzzing that Sir Bobby Robson had called him a good player.

He later went on to coach at Sheffield United and by now I had taken on the job as player liaison officer at Blackburn. One morning the phone went and he's telling me he'd just been for a run. This was after the back operation. He was telling me how he now didn't miss pre-season training. But he had been on a five-mile run and wanted me to guess what his time was for completing it. Considering the surgery etc, I went for around 35 minutes. Back came the reply: "30 minutes. I think I could still play, you know." This was after saying he was glad he wasn't playing anymore. He was now telling me he was capable of playing. I think he never ever wanted to stop being a player.

Looking back, it was obvious he needed to channel that disappointment at not being able to play any longer into something more positive. It didn't appear that going on to manage both Sheffield United and Wales was enough for him.

The first time our paths crossed was in my position as Bolton player liaison officer. We had just signed Speedo from Newcastle. With Speedo being 35, we only got permission to go ahead with the transfer because we were shown his Prozone stats for the season before with Newcastle, which as you can imagine were excellent. We met in the car park at Bolton's stadium. I took him up the M61 to the David Lloyd Centre for the medical. We quickly got chatting, had a few laughs before he did his fitness testing on the indoor tennis courts. I can still see him doing them now. I felt at ease with him straightaway. Some of the conversation was about cycling. I'm a massive cycling fan and the Tour de France was going on. He had been watching it as well. If I ever call in there – not that I go there that often now – I still see Speedo running around the tennis courts. Looking, as you can imagine, in peak condition.

He was a bit annoyed that Newcastle had decided to sell him. While he was conducting his fitness tests my phone rang and it was Big Sam. "Where the f*** are you?" he announced in that typical gruff manner. I told him I was with Speedo. "How much bloody longer has he got to go?" he enquired. I told him I didn't know. I wasn't a sports scientist! "Well," said Big Sam. "When he's finished don't let him ring anybody. Everton have come in for him and they are trying to nick him from me. I don't want to lose him so f***ing take his phone and don't let him take any calls. Get him back to me as soon as you can." He then promptly put the phone down.

Once Speedo had finished, I gave him back all his stuff but of course kept his phone in the bag. We're going back down the M61 and he turned to me and told me I could give the phone back to him. He said it would be all right. He already knew about Everton but he'd given his word to Big Sam and he wanted to join Bolton. So we arrived back at the Reebok for some soup and a sandwich and he saw Big Sam, and said he was signing because he had promised he would and liked what Bolton was all about.

He went back to his home that night and I texted him to

say how much I was looking forward to working with him. I was just having a quick beer and watching the Tour de France. He said he was watching it as well but he was drinking Champagne!

Although I got to like everything about him, I always called him 'Mournful'. "Morning Mournful," I used to say. Not many people around him appeared to pick up on the impression he gave me. I don't think with lots of people he allowed it to be seen. I think, for whatever reason, I was able to get under Speedo's skin. We had real heart-to-hearts driving in the car. At times really deep, dark conversations. I'd got into a spiral of problems and I think he could relate to them. I think my life would have been different if he hadn't have passed away. I don't think I would have got into the depths of despair which finally struck me. I would have gone to see him.

I'd lost my job at Blackburn – which I had brought on myself – and probably came close to a nervous breakdown. I was never an alcoholic but I wailing in self-pity and drinking far too much. If he had been alive that would never have happened because I would have gone to find him and he would have sorted me out. We had an innate understanding of each other's problems.

I still kick myself at times that I wasn't able to get to him before he did what he did. I should have gone to see him before I was due to meet up with him in Cardiff on the Monday. I had been worried with him telling me he was bored. How could he be with everything he had? Maybe I should have got in the car on that Thursday night straight after that telephone conversation.

He did have his dark moods. I can recall at Bolton we were

due to play at Ipswich Town in the FA Cup third round. In the lead-up to the game he was saying to me I had better tell the gaffer that he was no good coming off the substitutes' bench – he needed to start the game. Big Sam then called him in and said he could have the weekend off and that flattened him. He wanted to be told that Big Sam wanted him in the team at Ipswich – that the team couldn't do without him.

The gaffer did know how important he was but he wanted to rest him and save him for what he regarded as the more important league games.

My job is to look after players. It's what I'm doing now at Burnley. To be honest, I don't think football does enough when it comes down to players' welfare. The manager here, Sean Dyche, once described me as a person who cares about people in an industry that doesn't. I don't think there is that duty of care.

I still think to this day that Speedo made a terrible mistake by taking his own life. He wasn't a selfish man. He wouldn't have wanted people to suffer in the aftermath of his death.

If Speedo had mental problems he would never have admitted to them. In his early days at Bolton I would invite him back to my place for a meal. He'd get a taxi over. It could be a Champions League night. We would go to the local, have a couple of pints. Go back to the house, share a bottle of wine and we'd share a pasta bake and he would get a taxi back to his hotel. We enjoyed the time but maybe it was a couple of depressed idiots finding solace in each other.

I've since found a way to deal with my problems. It's all based on a healthy lifestyle, not drinking too much, eating the right things, exercising and reading quite a lot – keeping myself occupied. But the clouds are never far away. I almost lost one of my dogs in the summer and it placed me back in a spiral. You never know what's around the corner.

11

Louise's story

FINDING A WAY THROUGH

*'If he had witnessed the devastation and the
rippling effects it has left on so many people, I
can't imagine what he would be thinking. The
impact it has left is almost indescribable'*

Maybe it's my time now. I need to do something with
my life. I feel I've helped get the boys right. I've got
myself to a place of stability. I've got to find my
niche now. I've got another good 10-20 years or more in me,
hopefully. I'm afraid you never know what's around the corner
– that's the way I view life now. No-one knows what's in store
for you.

As far as Gary is concerned it's natural that everyone
wants to know why it happened. As I say, I haven't got
the answers. I'm supposed to have the answers but I
haven't. But I'm the one who has had to pick up the pieces

and carry on. I don't think people realise that but why should they?

For me, Gary went off to work, did a job and came home. He was my husband, the boy I met in school. It's as simple as that. Whether he had been a solicitor, accountant, a doctor or a builder, it wouldn't have mattered to me. That he chose to be a footballer was up to him. I didn't love him any more or any less because he was a footballer. Life in some ways was more tricky being with a footballer.

I can't complain because material-wise we've done well but then materials mean nothing when things like this happen. Everything else isn't important.

There have been a lot of dark times but the only thing that kept me going were the boys. Hearing them laugh again, having their friends around, having some great neighbours, it's what helped. I think in the first year you've got everyone around you and you keep busy. You are like a hot potato going from one thing to another. You are running on pure adrenaline.

The second year, when everyone else's life goes back to normal, you probably have the worst time. It really hits you and you experience some really low moments. With that in mind, I feel my recovery started the year after that.

I'm very proud of the boys and how they have coped with everything. Their take on life is be the best you can be. To take every opportunity you have and go for it.

We talk about their dad and the things we did together, the great times we had. We don't talk about why. It's just a chat about the nice times.

Both went over to the USA after finishing their schooling

here. Tommy first went off to Repton in Derbyshire to do his A-Levels.

I think the events surrounding Gary badly affected Ed's studying so he went down the college route to achieve the equivalent of A-Levels. Through their footballing ability they were both spotted by Neil Roberts, a former Wales international and a good friend of Gary's. He was working for Manchester City and part of his role involved inviting promising youngsters to study and play football in the USA. That's how they ended up in America.

Ed went to Herkimer College, New York, played his football and did well with his university course. He won some awards including being voted the college's male athlete of the year. Tommy had a gap year after completing his A-Levels and then got into a university called Adelphi on Long Island.

Ed has swapped universities and is now in Boston while Tommy is now in his second year at Adelphi. At the end of all this they will end up with scholarships, something to be very proud of. I think Ed would eventually love to go into football in some shape or form, whether it's coaching or playing. Tommy is open-minded, really. He is doing a business degree. He is enjoying his football but it's not the be-all and end-all for him.

The main thing is they are both enjoying life out there. You never know, one day we might be seeing one of them or both playing in the MLS [Major League Soccer]. It would be nice way to earn money, so who knows? There's a new club starting up in Miami with David Beckham. That would be nice!

It wasn't hard at all seeing them move there because I wanted them to get away from the media spotlight. It was a focus for me that they could spend a few years out there and be normal. At one stage I was thinking about moving there myself to get away from everything and everyone and start afresh.

I could have done it in the first year following Gary's passing but the boys didn't want to move away from our house in Chester. I could have done but they didn't want to. I found it incredibly difficult to remain there after what had happened. All I wanted was a fresh start. We would go away on holiday and then return to the house and I would take a deep breath and think, 'Here we go again back to it.'

It was strange because you half expected Gary to walk in though the backdoor to make everything normal again. At first, when the phone goes or there's a text message, you think it's from Gary. It was so surreal.

What had happened in my life had been so unpredictable and unreal that some days I've woken up thinking I don't want to be me today. I don't want to carry on. But we all miss him every day. It was so unnecessary. I think, could I have done more? What if this? What if that? What if he hadn't been a footballer?

Because of his strength of character is why he did what he did.

With Gary you try and try to get away from it but it's always there – a big scar inside you that will never disappear. It's tough. We had a lovely life. You can try and philosophise about it. The most certain thing in life is death and it's going to happen at some stage – but not usually like this.

Sadly, Ed's best mate at school also lost his father around six months after Gary died. The pair were real comforts for one another because of their mutual experience of losing their dad. The school also helped and I formed an even stronger friendship with Ed's friend's mother, Jill. It took a different route and it was based on something you would never want it to be based on. Again we helped each other. We can really relate to each other.

It's unbelievable this has happened to two families from the same school in such a short time. We have both moved on but there's still bewilderment for both of us. We've both gone through a rocky road with lots of bumps.

I wish Gary was here now to see how well the boys have done. He would be very proud of them. He has missed out on a lot, so much of their lives. We've missed out on him and gone through so much pain. It's something he obviously didn't think of at the time. If he had witnessed the devastation and the rippling effects it has left on so many people, I can't imagine what he would be thinking.

The impact it has left is almost indescribable. There is also so much love out there for him. It rips apart a large part of you which you can never replace because what happened was unnatural. That's when you realise it must be an illness because human nature is all about survival.

A couple of Christmases after Gary's death, I took the boys off to California to spend it with Warren and Candy Barton. Warren had been good friends with Gary at Newcastle and I got on well with Candy. They had both moved to San Diego and to be with them at such an emotional time of the year – and in the sunshine across the Atlantic – was really good for myself and the boys.

It did, for a time, make me think about whether I should

move to the USA. It would have meant getting away from what had gone on, a brand-new world. Nobody would know me or what I had gone through. It was continuous sunshine. The Bartons were great friends. It was a real pull at one point. I decided against it and remained in the Chester area.

As time goes by after the awful experience of the past, it's inevitable that you change as a person. You do act at first in a way that is not true to you. I eventually re-emerged as a slightly different person.

Everyone understandably asks why, why did it happen? There's also that part of me which asks, why me?

What is disappointing with what we know now is that Gary didn't ask for any support. For instance, he was a member of the League Managers Association, who supply whatever support you need in whatever form. I know that if anyone had come to Gary looking for advice – and they were a fellow manager – he would have recommended the LMA but it appears he didn't use them himself.

I will never forget the many, many – probably thousands – of letters of sympathy and support from all over the country. Many just arrived with 'Louise Speed, Chester' on the front of the envelopes but they got through to me. I eventually ended up reading every one of them. I've still got them.

To those wonderful people who thought about me at the time, I can't thank them enough. They meant so much to me and still do.

The Gary Speed MBE Playing Field

'This playing field is named in tribute to Gary Speed MBE who first played football here on his way to becoming a professional and international player and manager'

I

IN HIS OWN WORDS

'I always remember Howard Wilkinson said: "You've achieved more than anybody could imagine you have achieved so just don't think about anything else. Just go out and enjoy the last four or five games. You've got nothing to lose. Just go for it." That took all the pressure off us. We just went out and enjoyed it, where the pressure was on Man United so much you could see it.'

On the run-in for the 1992 league title

'I got a kick up my backside leaving Leeds to join Everton. Maybe it had come too easy for me early on. I love the place, I had a great time there, but being in a new environment, with a different viewpoint from people, made me quickly realise I wasn't as good as I thought I was.'

On leaving Leeds

'I never reacted at all to the flak and people can read into that what they like, but it was a privilege and an honour to play for Everton. The only time I'm not an Evertonian is in the 90 minutes I play against them. Everton are a very special club and joining them was the fulfilment of a dream for me. It is special to play for the team you supported as a boy, the team you watched from the terraces – it was a special feeling for me. Being captain was a tremendous honour, too. I will always remember when Howard Kendall told me I would be given the armband – it is something I could never forget.'

About his time at Goodison Park

'I'm not one for looking back and thinking, 'If only.' I left Everton under a cloud, as it were, and I think it would have been easy for me to have looked back and regretted moving to Newcastle, but while my proudest moment in football was captaining Wales and my happiest was winning the league title with Leeds, my happiest over a period of time was with Newcastle. I loved my time there – the club, the football we played, the city, the people.'

On his six-and-a-half years with the Magpies

'I will look back on landmarks when I retire and obviously I will have pride then, but I don't pay a lot *of attention to them at the moment. It makes me feel old, for starters, whenever people mention this record! I will hang my boots up one day and that will be the time to look back on what I've achieved, but not at the moment.'*

After becoming the first player to make 500 Premier League appearances while playing for Bolton

'From my point of view I could have won a bit more, and been a bit more successful in that respect, but I've got no regrets. I've had a great career and I've got a great life.'

Reflecting on the end of his playing career

'I am grateful and honoured to be in charge of a club with such great history and tradition, I would be a fool not to accept. The reason I want to be a manager is I wouldn't forgive myself if I hadn't given it a shot. I spoke to my wife briefly, but it wasn't really a discussion – she knew I was going to do it, so that was that, really. So she is going to be a long-suffering football manager's wife now!'

After stepping into the managerial hot seat at Sheffield United

'I was disappointed to leave Sheffield United because I feel I had unfinished business down there, but when your country comes calling, you don't turn them down. In my heart, I know this is absolutely the right decision. The proudest moment of my career was captaining Wales but being manager, the person responsible for the team, will eclipse even that. Having this job is the greatest honour I could have and I'm going to do everything I can to make a success of it. It is my biggest regret in football that I never reached the finals of a major tournament, so the opportunity to try to put that right and achieve that feat with my country as manager is a challenge I'm ready to embrace with open arms.'

After taking the Wales manager's job

'I would not have got into this Welsh team – I would not have been good enough. I'm being absolutely serious. There is quality in this team, from goalkeeper through to centre-forward, which potentially exceeds any Welsh team I have known. They play magnificently together and will get better and better. There are classier players in this team than I ever was and hopefully this is the group who will finally get Wales to one of these major finals. That is certainly my aim.'

After Wales beat Norway 4-1
in his final match in charge

//

TRIBUTES TO SPEEDO

'Gary is missed hugely by everyone. He was intelligent, witty and very, very down to earth despite his success as a footballer and manager of Wales.'

Alan Shearer

'As soon as he arrived at school you could see his potential talent on the football field. We had an annual challenge match between the staff and the pupils and at half-time we realised we just couldn't cope with him. His movement, his speed, I think we had to resort to some unfair tactics – let's put it that way – to try to curb his forward runs!'

Paul Ellis, Gary's former teacher
at Hawarden High School

'I was proud of Gary Speed, like a kind of father figure would be, because he wasn't the most talented of kids when I first met him but he wanted to make himself better. I am going to miss his laugh, he had a childlike laugh. I was speaking to Gary McAllister and I said I would forget the games and the goals but I would never forget his laugh, and I am never going to hear that again.'

Gordon Strachan

'He was a smashing lad. He was a very respected man in and around football, not only for his ability but for the guy as a person. I signed Gary for £5 million from Everton and he did a fantastic job for us at Newcastle.'

Kenny Dalglish

'Gary was one of the ultimate professionals at Newcastle and a shining example to his younger colleagues. He was an inspiration to all of those around him and a true football person as well as a great friend of mine. He was regarded in the game as one of the true greats – and always will be.'

John Carver

'He will be a miss in the dressing room, he will be a miss in the training room, he will be a miss in the restaurants, he will be a miss on the planes, on the buses, in every concept imaginable of that boy coming in to play football for Newcastle and departing, he will be a miss.'

Bobby Robson following Gary's departure for Bolton

'He wasn't just a great player, he was a great person, too. He was always great to be around, the life and soul of the party, and a good friend.'

Rob Lee

'Gary Speed was one of the nicest men in football and someone I am honoured to call a team-mate and friend.'

Ryan Giggs

'I was fortunate to take Gary to Bolton. At that stage he was a young 34 and most people were saying he was getting past it, but in actual fact his stats were absolutely outstanding. As soon as he walked into the club he had an aura. He did everything to detail. When generally an old professional might moan and groan and say "I don't want to do this" he just took it on board. I was also fortunate to get to know him as a person. He was an outstanding individual and this is what's devastating. His life was about standards, he had a high standard for everything that he did. To sum it up, if you had a daughter and she brought Gary Speed home, you'd be delighted.'

Sam Allardyce

'I played with him and I knew him as a colleague for many years. He was captain of Wales when the likes of Mark Hughes and Ian Rush were still playing and I think that tells you a lot about the man he was. I can't put into words what a fantastic guy he was. In that short space of time [with Wales] he showed the talent he had for working with the players. He had such a bright, fantastic future to look forward to.'

Mark Bowen, Gary's former team-mate and assistant manager with Wales

'I think if you've ever been in Gary's company, what struck you was his manner and the way he conducted himself. You felt that you were in the company of somebody special.'

Mark Hughes

'When we went through the selection process, Gary wasn't necessarily the most experienced manager there but he had some fantastic qualities. He was a true professional, a fantastic gentleman and he got the players where they wanted to be, they wanted to play for him and it wasn't just players – it was the fans, the staff, everybody around him. It's such a sad loss.'

Jonathan Ford, Chief Executive of the Football Association of Wales

'Gary was a wonderful ambassador for our league, and indeed all of football, but more than that he was a decent man widely respected throughout the game and beyond. Gary will go down in history as one of our iconic players.'

Richard Scudamore, Executive Chairman of the Premier League

'Gary had a great career in management ahead of him. He would have been one the best. Gary had a different philosophy and a different way as a manager. He was sharp and clever.'

Rob Earnshaw, former Wales international

'At 42 and with a wife and two young children, the futility and senselessness of Gary Speed's death is undeniable, but the game will continue because, unfortunately, that is how it is. Football is a tough sport and there really is no support network for those who are troubled or in need of help. The minute you walk out of any club, you are gone forever.'

Alan Hansen, Liverpool legend and retired Match Of The Day pundit

'He was rare in football. It's a jealous world, people are always having a go at you or talking about someone, but you never heard Gary Speed talking about anybody or anybody saying anything bad about him. When someone dies people always say nice things but genuinely, I don't think there's anyone in the game who had any edge with Speedo.'

Paul Jewell, who did his coaching badges with Gary

'The world has lost a great football manager but even more sadly a great man.'

Aaron Ramsey, who was appointed Wales' youngest-ever captain by Gary

'Being with him that day at Football Focus, 20 minutes before going on air, he was the normal Gary Speed, the guy I've known for a long, long time – looking class, immaculately presented, as he always is. He's a movie star in my eyes. There were no signs. Nothing would suggest he was troubled. Things were going well for him.'

Gary McAllister

///

A GLITTERING CAREER

Leeds United

1988–1996

Gary's qualities as a midfielder were abundantly clear from an early age and when he caught the eye of Howard Wilkinson at Leeds United, few were surprised when the Welshman immediately settled into the first XI despite being just 19 years of age.

He benefitted from the expertise of those around him, learning from the likes of Gordon Strachan, Gary McAllister and David Batty as the Elland Road outfit won the Second Division title in 1990, before the energetic youngster played a huge role in further success in west Yorkshire.

In the final year of English top-flight football before the

advent of the Premier League, Wilkinson led Leeds United to the First Division title, an accolade that Gary played a huge hand in.

Fending off Sir Alex Ferguson's Manchester United, Leeds won the title by four points, with Speed scoring six league goals and a further three in the League Cup to underline his worth to Wilkinson's side.

The 1991-92 season would prove to be a nadir for Gary at Elland Road but he remained with the club until the end of the 1995-96 season, a tenure that cemented his affections with Leeds fans forever.

Everton

1996–1998

When Gary's boyhood idols Everton showed an interest in the midfielder, it was quickly clear he would be moving to Merseyside in no time at all.

Everton manager Joe Royle took him to Goodison Park in a £3.5 million deal. His finest moment in a Royal Blue shirt came with a hat-trick in a 7-1 victory over Southampton in the 1996-97 season.

Everton manager Royle regarded him as the lynchpin of his side and Gary more than played a part in fending off relegation as his goal against Tottenham Hotspur – a flying header no less – enabled Everton to escape the drop that season.

Gary's commitment, fitness and accurate passing game, plus

his clear delight in playing for the club he supported, ensured he was also voted Player of the Year in 1996-97.

At the start of the following campaign, Howard Kendall – the club's legendary 1980s manager – returned to the Everton dugout and immediately made Gary the club captain, a just reward for his performances the season before.

However, Newcastle United were soon to come calling and, amid controversial circumstances in February 1998, he was on his way to join Kenny Dalglish in the North East.

In a short statement to the Liverpool Echo, he said: "You know why I'm leaving, but I can't explain myself publicly because it would damage the good name of Everton Football Club and I'm not prepared to do that."

Newcastle United

1998–2004

It was in the North East that Gary arguably enjoyed the most high-profile years of his career.

Surrounded by the likes of Shay Given, Alan Shearer, Warren Barton and Keith Gillespie, he quickly established himself as a leader and lynchpin in the Newcastle side and his fee of £5.5 million felt like good value for a player who may have been playing top-class football for a decade already but who was someone clearly capable and competitive enough to remain at the highest level for some time to come.

Gary was a true leader at St. James' Park, captaining the

side in the absence of local hero Shearer, and although two consecutive FA Cup final appearances – in 1998 and 1999 – both ended in defeat, the Magpies became a force to be reckoned with during the Welshman's stay and he enjoyed two Champions League campaigns with the club.

The midfielder played under three managers at Newcastle – Kenny Dalglish, Ruud Gullit and Sir Bobby Robson – and all three publicly praised his work ethic, the self-discipline he showed with his fitness and training and his tremendous desire to succeed.

Bolton Wanderers

2004–2008

Gary's exit from Newcastle came as a huge surprise to many at the club, who felt they would sorely lack his leadership qualities.

He moved to North West side Bolton Wanderers and while many players approaching 35 would have been tempted by retirement, the Welshman wanted to demonstrate he still had plenty to offer.

Bolton manager Sam Allardyce wanted experience and top-flight know-how in his side and he could scarcely have recruited a better player, with Gary complimenting the likes of Jay-Jay Okocha, Fernando Hierro and Ivan Campo as one of the older heads in the dressing room.

Yet Gary proved that age is just a number during his time

at the Reebok Stadium – as it was then known – and helped his unfashionable club finish sixth in his first season, eighth and then seventh as Bolton managed to continue to confound budgets and expectations and remain a comfortable Premier League side.

Sheffield United

2008–2010 (player, coach and manager)

Gary joined the Blades at the start of 2008 – in fact he played on New Year's Day for his new club, the day he signed – but his playing time at Bramall Lane was curtailed by a back injury.

Bryan Robson had convinced Speed to join United but he was swiftly replaced as manager by Kevin Blackwell, who encouraged the midfielder, now 38, to pursue a dual role as part of his backroom staff.

Eventually, he required surgery due to a disc problem in his back, and it was this injury that ultimately ended his playing career.

However, he thrived in his coaching role, obtaining the Uefa Pro Licence during his recuperation, and was offered the manager's job following Blackwell's departure early into the 2009-10 season.

He would spend only four months in the position before leaving to take on the challenge of trying to lead Wales to a major tournament for the first time since 1958.

Wales

1990–2004 (player)
2010–2011 (manager)

Gary's last match in charge of the national team came more than two decades after he made his senior Wales debut.

He first pulled on the red shirt on May 20, 1990, coming on as a substitute in a 1-0 friendly win against Costa Rica at Ninian Park.

It wasn't long before he became one of the first names on the Wales team sheet and his leadership qualities were rewarded in 1998 when he was appointed captain by Bobby Gould.

He ended his international playing career six years later with 85 caps, a record for a Welsh outfield player, and seven goals.

A member of the teams that recorded famous victories over Germany, Brazil and Italy, Gary was disappointed not to appear in a major finals but aimed to put that right after stepping into the managerial hot seat in December 2010.

He oversaw a renaissance in the team's fortunes, with four wins in five matches propelling Wales 72 places up the world rankings, just three months after dropping to an all-time low of 117.

Gary's final match was the 4-1 friendly win over Norway at the Cardiff City Stadium on November 12, 2011.

Wales would reach the semi-finals of Euro 2016 under Chris Coleman's leadership, and the groundwork for that success was laid by the man from Flintshire.

Chris Brereton

Playing career statistics

Leeds United
Signed: June 13, 1988
Debut: May 6, 1989, Football League Second Division,
(H) v Oldham Athletic, drew 0-0
Last match: April 30, 1996, Premier League,
(H) v Newcastle United, lost 0-1

Stats	Apps	Sub	Goals
League	231	17	39
FA Cup	21	0	5
League Cup	25	1	11
Other cups	14	3	2
Total	291	21	57

Honours
First Division championship 1991-92
League Cup runner-up 1996

Everton
Signed: July 1, 1996, £3.5 million transfer fee
Debut: August 17, 1996, Premier League,
(H) v Newcastle United, won 2-0 (scored one goal)
Last match: January 18, 1998, Premier League,
(H) v Chelsea, won 3-1 (scored one goal)

Stats	Apps	Sub	Goals
League	58	0	16
FA Cup	2	0	1
League Cup	5	0	1
Other cups	0	0	0
Total	65	0	18

Newcastle United

Signed: February 6, 1998, £5.5 million transfer fee
Debut: February 7, 1998, Premier League,
(H) v West Ham United, lost 1-0
Last match: May 15, 2004, Premier League,
(A) v Liverpool, drew 1-1

Stats	Apps	Sub	Goals
League	206	7	29
FA Cup	22	0	5
League Cup	9	2	1
Other cups	39	0	5
Total	276	9	40

Honours
FA Cup runner-up 1998
FA Cup runner-up 1999

Bolton Wanderers

Signed: July 21, 2004, £750,000 transfer fee
Debut: August 14, 2004, Premier League,
(H) v Charlton Athletic, won 4-1
Last match: December 9, 2007, Premier League,
(H) v Wigan Athletic, won 4-1

Stats	Apps	Sub	Goals
League	115	6	14
FA Cup	6	0	0
League Cup	4	0	0
Other cups	5	3	0
Total	130	9	14

Sheffield United

Signed: January 1, 2008, £250,000 transfer fee
Debut: January 1, 2008, Championship, (A) v Wolves, drew 0-0
Last match: November 25, 2008, Championship,
(H) v Wolves, lost 1-3

Stats	Apps	Sub	Goals
League	37	0	6
FA Cup	2	0	0
League Cup	1	0	0
Other cups	0	0	0
Total	40	0	6

Wales

Under-21s: 3 appearances, 0 goals
Senior debut: May 8, 1990, friendly, (H) v Costa Rica, won 1-0
Last match: October 13, 2004, World Cup qualifier,
(H) v Poland, lost 2-3

Playing career record:

Stats	Apps	Sub	Goals
Club career	802	39	135
Wales	85	5	7

Premier League's top 20 appearance makers:

	Player	Apps		Player	Apps
1	Gareth Barry	653	10	Steven Gerrard	504
2	Ryan Giggs	632	12	Sol Campbell	503
3	Frank Lampard	609	13	Paul Scholes	499
4	David James	572	14	Jermain Defoe	492
5	**Gary Speed**	**535**	14	John Terry	492
6	Emile Heskey	516	16	Wayne Rooney	491
7	Mark Schwarzer	514	17	James Milner	485
8	Jamie Carragher	508	18	Michael Carrick	481
9	Phil Neville	505	19	Sylvain Distin	469
10	Rio Ferdinand	504	20	Peter Crouch	462

Stats correct up to the start of the 2018-19 Premier League season

Management career statistics

Sheffield United
Appointed: August 17, 2010
First match: August 22, Championship,
(A) v Middlesbrough, lost 0-1
Last match: December 11, 2010, Championship,
(A) v Barnsley, lost 0-1

Stats	Played	Won	Drew	Lost
League	18	6	3	9

Wales
Appointed: December 14, 2010
First match: February 8, 2011, Four Nations,
(A) v Republic of Ireland, lost 0-3
Last match: December 12, 2011, friendly,
(H) v Norway, won 4-1

Stats	Played	Won	Drew	Lost
Euro 2012 qualifying	5	3	0	2
Four Nations tournament	3	1	0	2
Friendly	2	1	0	1
Total	10	5	0	5

Wales 4-1 Norway

*In his final game in charge of Wales, Gary oversaw
an impressive victory against Norway in Cardiff,
and here we reproduce the match report which
originally featured on WalesOnline*

On the eve of Remembrance Sunday, Gary Speed's increasingly impressive Wales team served up a performance to live long in the memory of the 12,673 Wales fans at the Cardiff City Stadium today.

Gary Speed's resurgent young outfit have now firmly established themselves as the team nobody wants to face first when the World Cup 2014 fixtures are drawn up later this month.

After brushing Egil Olsen's experienced Norway team aside in the opening 16 minutes, Speed's forward quartet of Gareth Bale, Craig Bellamy, Aaron Ramsey and Steve Morison must now be among the most feared in Europe as the impressive team finished a rout against the team ranked 24 in the world.

Tottenham star Bale was first on the act, banishing thoughts of his controversial Team GB 2012 Olympics marketing involvement, to hold his nerve and fire firmly past Norway goalkeeper Rune Jarstein from a seemingly impossible left hand angle on 11 minutes.

It seemed as though the improved Cardiff City Stadium crowd was still in celebration mode when the team's elder statesman Craig Bellamy picked the ball up on halfway and drove forward before unleashing a curling shot just inside Jarsein's other post from 25 yards.

As Bellamy celebrated his 19th goal for Wales (his first in eight internationals) at the stadium where he impressed so much while playing on loan last season, the home fans were in dreamland.

From then on, led by the impressive Ramsey and his midfield partner Joe Allen, Wales controlled the game, only troubled briefly by a rasping Mohammed Abdellaoue strike which rebounded back off the post, allowing Wales' relieved goalkeeper Wayne Hennessey to get to half-time without making a notable save.

But in the second half, spurred on by substitutes Vadim Demidov and Simen Brenner, Norway edged back into the game when towering Portsmouth striker Erik Huseklepp latched onto some sloppy defending involving Hennessey and centre-back Darcy Blake to fire into an empty net six yards out.

Unperturbed by the uncharacteristic lapse, man-of-the-match Bellamy and Bale spurred the Dragons forward to keep testing Norway's experienced back four, which included the 170 combined caps of Bellamy's old adversary John Arne Riise and his Fulham team-mate Brede Hangeland.

The effervescent Liverpool forward was a constant thorn in the Scandinavian's side, winning a string of corners out of Kjetil Waehler in the first half and Vadim Demidov in the second.

With 20 minutes to go, the emergence of Wolves target man Sam Vokes, who replaced the tiring Steve Morison up front, moved Wales up another gear.

Vokes' first goal put the result beyond doubt when more great work from Bale and Bellamy put the tall striker in on the far post in front of the excited fans in the Canton Stand.

Then moments later, the same man fired in an even more impressive right footed strike from outside the box to finish off the hammering Wales deserved to dish out.

IV

HEADS TOGETHER

Louise Speed bravely contributed to this book because she wanted to help make a difference to others who may be suffering in the same way as Gary. Louise nominated the Heads Together campaign which helps tackle the stigma around mental health.

Heads Together is spearheaded by Prince Harry and the Duke and Duchess of Cambridge, who used their Royal Foundation to launch the initiative in 2016. It unites several of the country's leading mental health charities, including Best Beginnings, CALM – The Campaign Against Living Miserably, Contact, Place2Be, The Mix, YoungMinds and Mind. They all want to ensure the right help is available to anyone seeking mental health support, wherever they are and whenever they need it.

As part of the campaign, the royals commissioned 10 films of celebrities discussing their mental health issues and how talking about them made a huge difference. Among those who opened up about the problems they had faced were former England cricket captain Andrew Flintoff, rapper Professor Green and comic Ruby Wax.

Harry himself has spoken about "shutting down" his feelings after his mother, Princess Diana, died when he was 12 years old. The Prince revealed he later sought therapy and took up boxing to combat his frustration.

Money raised by Heads Together, which was made the 2017 Virgin Money London Marathon Charity of the Year, is now supporting innovative projects to tackle the challenges people face in talking about our mental health.

This includes a £2 million fund to create digital tools for young people seeking help online and new programmes to support mental health in schools, workplaces and the armed forces community.

"Through our work with young people, emergency response, homeless charities, and veterans, we have seen time and time again that unresolved mental health problems lie at the heart of some of our greatest social challenges," the charity says.

"Too often, people feel afraid to admit that they are struggling with their mental health. This fear of prejudice and judgement stops people from getting help and can destroy families and end lives. Heads Together wants to help people feel much more comfortable with their everyday mental wellbeing and have the practical tools to support their friends and family."

For more information about the Heads Together campaign,
visit www.headstogether.org.uk.

A note from CALM
(The Campaign Against Living Miserably)

A substantial donation from the proceeds of the hardback edition of this book has been made to CALM. This was made at the request of Louise Speed.

The Campaign Against Living Miserably (CALM) is leading a movement against suicide, the single biggest killer of men under 45 in the UK.

Our approach to tackling this issue is two-fold. Firstly, we provide support for anyone who is going through a difficult time with our free, anonymous and confidential helpline and webchat which are open every day, 5pm–midnight. We also support those bereaved by suicide through the Support After Suicide Partnership – hosted by CALM.

Secondly, we work with the whole of society – through cultural touchpoints like music, comedy, sport and fashion – to raise awareness of this issue and provide support solutions that can enable us to better look after ourselves and those around us. Our campaigns always have service provision at their heart and aim to open up the conversation around mental health, suicide, and the damaging masculine stereotypes that can often prevent people from seeking support when they need it most.

We're hugely grateful to Louise and the team behind this vital book for their support of CALM. Projects like this allow us to continue supporting any man who may be going through a tough time.

Find out more about CALM and join the movement against suicide at thecalmzone.net.